PEGGED DOWN

EXPERIENCES OF PEOPLE IN IRELAND WITH SIGNIFICANT PHYSICAL DISABILITIES

JEAN TUBRIDY

First published 1996
by the Institute of Public Administration,
57-61 Lansdowne Road,
Dublin 4, Ireland.

British Library Cataloguing in Publication Data

ISBN 1 872002 53 6

Cover Design by Creative Image Associates
Typeset by Peanntrónaic Teoranta
Printed by ColourBooks Ltd

*To my parents
and Adrian and Harry*

ACKNOWLEDGEMENTS

I would like to thank very sincerely all those who have made this publication possible. The most significant contribution was made by the thirty people with disabilities and their relatives who provided the data on which the book is based. They were extremely helpful and supportive of the research and my hope is that this book will go some way towards developing the kind of public understanding of the requirements and aspirations of people with disabilities, which they wanted so badly.

Special thanks are due to Professor John Jackson of the Sociology Department, Trinity College, Dublin, who was such a helpful supervisor while I was writing the doctoral thesis on which this book is based. I would like to acknowledge generous assistance provided by APT, Tullamore; The Rehab Foundation; and the National Rehabilitation Board, assistance which has been vital in enabling this book to be published.

I am most grateful to my colleagues Ann Byrne-Lynch and Margaret Hodgins, in the SENSES Network, who were always there with words of encouragement when I needed them. Denis Doherty, CEO of the Midland Health Board has also been very supportive about the idea of publishing this material.

Finally, I want to thank Tony McNamara of the Institute of Public Administration with whom it has been such a pleasure to work.

CONTENTS

INTRODUCTION

This book is about the experiences of people with physical disabilities in Ireland over the years since the late 1930s. It opens up a section of our social history which has remained virtually unexplored for all sorts of reasons, including public ignorance, fear and discomfort regarding 'the disabled'.

The whole thrust of formal social policy in Ireland has in recent decades shifted away from excluding people with disabilities towards including them to the greatest extent possible into the life of the community. This philosophy has underpinned stated objectives relating to various dimensions of life such as education, employment, living arrangements and leisure.

What is surprising, in view of the ongoing emphasis on inclusion, is that there is such a dearth of published material on the experiences of people with physical disabilities in this country. This book seeks to help fill that gap. It gives the outside world an opportunity to learn about the realities of life and the needs, hopes and fears of people with physical disabilities. It is also a vehicle through which people with physical disabilities have a chance to express themselves and to present their experiences and opinions. This is an opportunity which they have traditionally been denied, either because it was assumed that they could not speak for themselves or that able-bodied professionals knew better.

The book is based on extracts from tape-recorded

interviews with thirty adults who have physical disabilities. How were these people selected from the many thousands in Ireland who have some form of physical disability? An essential point here is that a decision was made from the outset to try to take account of two key variables associated with disabling conditions which could well be expected to influence people's experience of disability. The first of these relates to the age at which a person becomes disabled and more specifically to whether he or she has grown up with the disability or acquired it after years of experiencing life as a non-disabled person. The second variable relates to the prognosis associated with disabling conditions and, crucially, to whether they are progressive or non-progressive. Three disabling conditions were identified in which the congenital/acquired and progressive/non-progressive dimensions were combined in different ways. These were as follows:

- **cerebral palsy** – onset in infancy or early childhood / non-progressive

- **traumatic spinal cord injury in adulthood** – onset in adulthood/non-progressive

- **multiple sclerosis** – onset in adulthood/ progressive.

So, the group of thirty was divided equally between people who were disabled due to one of these three relatively common conditions. (The main features associated with cerebral palsy, spinal cord injury and multiple sclerosis are outlined in the Appendix.) Six other criteria were used in selecting people to participate in the study. They had to be:

- restricted in their ability to walk to the extent that they either used a wheelchair or would be expected to do so

- aged between twenty-five and fifty-five at the time of interview
- affected by their disabling condition for at least five years
- of 'normal' intelligence
- able to communicate
- resident in Dublin City or County.

The fact that there is no general register of people with physical disabilities in Ireland made the task of finding people who met these criteria quite daunting. It seemed important to ensure that people from all types of social background could be included in the study so that the full range of experience of those with physical disabilities could be explored. Because of this, it seemed inappropriate to work through, e.g. the Irish Wheelchair Association and the Multiple Sclerosis Society, since not everyone chooses to become a member of these organisations. The approach which appeared to be most suitable was to work through the patient lists of medical specialists who were involved with people affected by cerebral palsy, multiple sclerosis and spinal cord injury. This was because practically all those who are diagnosed as having one of these conditions would have been seen by a medical specialist at some stage and this, in turn, would have led to the opening of a patient file.

It proved possible to secure people with cerebral palsy and multiple sclerosis using the patient files of medical specialists. However, alternative arrangements had to be made in relation to those with spinal cord injuries and they were found with the assistance of the National Rehabilitation Board.

The eventual participants in the study were chosen using

a process of random selection from the relevant lists of people who met the criteria which had been set down. Care was taken to ensure that the overall distribution of each condition by sex would be reflected in the groups selected for the study. Thus, males outnumbered females in both the spinal cord injury and the cerebral palsy groups and females outnumbered males in the multiple sclerosis group.

The interviews with the thirty people in the study were held during the mid-1980s at locations of their choice and in most cases this was in their own homes. The meetings were quite informal and the average length of time spent with each person was three and a half hours, spread over two sessions. It was intended from the outset that the interviews should remain relatively unstructured so that the people with physical disabilities would have the opportunity to identify those issues which had emerged as being of particular concern to them during their lives. Consequently, although each person was asked to talk about his or her experiences in relation to the same set of broad subject areas such as education and employment, they had a good deal of control over the general direction which the interviews took.

It was planned from the beginning to hold interviews with the parents of those with cerebral palsy so that information could be gathered about the early years of their children's lives. It proved possible to meet with parents, mainly the mothers, of six of the ten people in the study. It should also be mentioned here that there were a few cases in which spouses of the people with physical disabilities were present during interviews. Their comments have also been included at various points throughout the book as they offer yet another perspective on the experience of living with disability. The transcriptions of the interviews filled a total of almost nine hundred pages. All the material is very rich and it has been difficult to edit it down for publication. Throughout this task, the main objective has been to give as fair a representation as possible of the range of experiences and views which emerged from the interviews as a whole. The emphasis in this study has been on the personal viewpoints of people with disabilities and it should be recognised that these may not be accurate at all times especially where there is a reliance on long-term memory.

The chapters which follow trace the experiences of the thirty people in the study over their careers since the onset of disability. Considerable care has been taken to conceal the identities of those who participated in the interviews. In particular, their names and various other details surrounding their lives have been altered.

In view of the fact that the interviews used in this book were held in the mid-1980s, an Epilogue has been included which sets out all the main developments that have taken place in the physical disability field during the past ten years.

CHAPTER 1

WHAT'S WRONG WITH ME?

For most people, the process of becoming physically disabled is a journey into the unknown. Nobody really knows how they will cope with it until they are actually faced with the uncertainties and the challenges which it involves. This chapter is concerned with the first direct experiences of physically disabling conditions and the ways in which those affected learned of what exactly the doctors thought was wrong with them.

'You don't send for it'

There are many different ways in which disability can strike. It can enter a person's life very suddenly, creep up insidiously over a long period, or steer a course somewhere between these two extremes. Its arrival is very seldom welcomed and, as we shall see, disability can place enormous demands on the time and energy of those whose lives it invades.

The people in the study who were most certain about the precise time at which they had acquired their disabilities were those who had suffered spinal cord injuries. Gerry was very succinct about his particular experience:

> I was twenty-one going on twenty-two when I had my smash, a car crash. Rolling down a hill and the brakes failed in the car at around 8.30 or 9.30 in the evening. Complete brake failure – just one of those things. If it sounds blasé, it's after the mists of mellow fruitlessness fifteen years hence.

Eddie, whose motorbike accident had occurred six years before the time of interview, had a vivid recollection of his various actions and thoughts at the time of the accident:

> So, I was coming up and round a bend. And I just saw one of these red bricks just right on the bend and I was leaning into the bend. Course, I couldn't avoid the brick so I just barely twisted the steering, didn't use any brakes at all. And didn't the brick hit the wheel. Whatever way it jumped, it straightened up and went out of control completely. Hit the only pole that was on the corner. So bang, crash. That was it. Lying on the ground then. The ambulance was out fair enough a few minutes after. The usual, they were cutting all the clothes off me. They were saying about the leg, 'It's going to hurt a bit.' So I felt it strange – Jasus, I didn't feel a thing. I never thought, like, you know. You'd just think it was a broken leg and that was it.

Accidents involving motor vehicles and falls are the two most common causes of spinal cord injuries. The experience of those in the study followed this broad pattern. Two were driving cars when their accidents occurred and one was driving a motorbike. Three were passengers in cars which crashed and one was injured in a hit-and-run accident involving a car. The other three were all injured as a result of falls. Six of the ten said that their accidents had involved excessive drinking. Paddy was among these:

> It was a Friday night and like any other Friday night after knocking off work – I used to meet the boss and go out for a jar. That morning he'd left the keys on the fridge. So when we came back to his place we were sitting on the wall – there's a kind of parapet and steps leading to the house – and I was sitting on that and Jimmy was trying to open the door. And I was laughing so much at his antics trying to open the door. So he came across and gave me a belt across the head with the keys and I fell back down into the basement and I broke me spine.

Some of the people who had multiple sclerosis felt they could identify exactly when they had first been affected by the disease. For example, Elaine said:

> I was perfect until I was sixteen. Then slapbang my eyesight goes for about three to four months. Then it came back double which is worse. Then it came back perfect.

However, others with multiple sclerosis found it difficult to pinpoint the precise time when they had their first episode of the disease. Helen was fairly typical of these:

> My husband got an awful crock when he got me because when I was about two years married my health started to go. I developed pneumonia and out of that I got asthma and I was going around with an inhaler. I was like that for so many years and then I started to get these different impaired feelings and dropping things. I didn't say anything to my husband for a long, long time and I was playing around with the idea that I had a tumour on the brain. Then I started this falling business and no matter what was on the floor, even a thread,

I'd blame it for knocking me. Then I seen a difference in my eye. It was kind of dropped a bit. It got all right itself. The next thing was I got double vision. I was taken in and I had a lumbar puncture and I believe it was then my husband was told I had MS.

The first realisation that those who were later diagnosed as having cerebral palsy might not be developing normally did not occur until the children were aged between eight months and two years. The main signs which began causing concern among the parents were that their children were slow, compared to other babies, in such activities as holding their bottles, sitting up and talking. In Paula's case, it was her aunt who first suspected that something was wrong:

They didn't realise it until I was old enough to eat an apple and my aunt came over and she put one in my hand. You know the way a child automatically puts anything they get into their hands straight into their mouth. I didn't. My hands just stayed where they were. She was the one to discover it. It was then she said to my parents that there was something. I think that was one of the reasons that my father did not like my aunt cos she was the one that found out that there was something.

Eight of those with cerebral palsy were able to point to what they felt were the likely causes of their condition. Dave and Derek said that the use of forceps during their deliveries, coupled with the inexperience of the doctors involved, was the likely cause of their having cerebral palsy. Derek was still quite bitter about this:

It was just one of those things – an accident. The doctor made a mistake. He squeezed the forceps too tightly – his first delivery.

Both Christine and Paula suspected that the fact that they had been premature babies had caused them to have cerebral palsy. Christine, who was an only child, also pointed to the fact that her mother had had a very bad history in trying to have children:

> My mother had five other children. There were two born dead and the rest were miscarriages. I was a six months baby, two and a half pounds when I was born, and my mother was given no hope for me at all. I was in an incubator for almost a year. Then they took me home and my mother did not discover that there was anything wrong with me at that stage.

The other suspected causes of disability were: a mother's fall during pregnancy; a very quick delivery at home; an extremely complicated and lengthy delivery; the baby being three weeks overdue. There was no obvious reason why either Paul or Jane had been affected by cerebral palsy. However, Paul's mother seemed to suspect an element of divine intervention:

> I mean it's God's will, isn't it? You don't send for it.

It is often said that there is much ignorance about disability among the able-bodied population in Ireland. The people who participated in the study certainly felt that this was the case and almost all of them drew attention to the fact that they themselves had been very ignorant about disability until it entered their own lives. Paul's mother, for example, spoke of how inadequate she had felt when she had learned his diagnosis:

> My sister round the corner had a child actually three days after I had him. That was the only way I could make a

5

comparison with how he was and he didn't sit up the way she sat up. It wasn't until he was fifteen months.old and I was minding him all the time without nobody telling me anything. He took a fit. I sent for my GP and it was him said, 'He's spastic.' I thought spastic was something you could eat. I hadn't a clue and I said, 'What will I do?' He said, 'I suppose you could bring him to Doctor Brown.'

Deirdre had had a similar sort of experience when she was told that she had multiple sclerosis:

The doctor sat back and he said, 'Mrs Nolan, you have multiple sclerosis,' like he got an awful shock. Says I, 'Is that all, doctor?' never dreaming, never knowing what it was.

The various people with spinal injury said that, before their own accidents, they had been oblivious to the fact that an injury to the spinal cord could have such an impact on a person's life. For example, Eoin said:

This is how ignorant I was. I didn't even know I had a spinal cord. I was never really taught anything like that at school. I was never taught these things. I was very interested in biological things but mostly sort of like in flowers you'd learn about in school for exams. I got to the spinal cord all right but I never really understood. I never knew I had a spinal cord or that you can go out there and ruin yourself for life.

Danny pointed out that he had never realised that it was possible to have a serious spinal injury and still live:

I always thought if you broke your neck that you died because all the cowboys used to fall off their horses and break their necks. Seriously, it's only since the 1960s that they started keeping broken necks alive. You realise that?

'Well, that was the hurting point anyway'

Some of the most emotional and heartfelt statements which were made by the people in the study arose in relation to their experiences of learning their diagnoses. The crucial significance of learning one's diagnosis and the future outlook is that it introduces an element of certainty into what has often become an almost unbearable sea of speculation, characterised by conflicting surges of hope and desperation. Danny, who was paralysed from the neck down as a result of a car crash, described the onset of this certainty in a very vivid way:

> I just don't remember a lot of it for the first month and then it was after about a month lying in the ward. I remember we were all having a conversation in the ward. Incredible thing, you just hear voices coming from all the beds. I remember just lying there one night, seeing a bloke pushing himself through the ward and it dawned on me, 'There's no turning back now; there's no going back to the life you had.' There's no one ever turns round and says to you, 'You'll never walk again,' and all this sort of nonsense. That's all in fairy books. That's not real life at all. The doctor doesn't have to say, 'You'll never walk again,' cos you know it. No one ever said to me I'd never walk again but I knew it.

There are many ways in which people can learn that either they themselves or a member of their family have a seriously disabling condition. A common way in which those in the study learned theirs was through being told directly by a doctor soon after the diagnosis had actually been made. Conor, who was one of the most disabled people with spinal cord injury, had a vivid recollection of the moment when his doctor told him of the extent of his injuries:

> It was only when I was out in the big ward and I saw a few wheelchairs around, something was telling me. But as far as I was concerned I was just there and my legs were tired. I asked the doctor point blank out, 'What's the chances of walking again?' 'Oh,' he said, 'there's no chance of it.' Well, that was the hurting point anyway.

Jane's mother could also remember clearly the way a specialist had told herself and her husband of their daughter's diagnosis some thirty years earlier:

> At nine or ten months when she wasn't sitting up we went to a lady doctor – I forget her name – and she diagnosed her that she had cerebral palsy. But she broke it very gently, that so much could be done and so in other words we were going from year to year not letting it worry us. She didn't frighten us and say, 'You are going to have a handicapped child.' That was a great help because you know when you are younger and that I think the shock would have been terrific if she had come in and said, 'Listen, you are going to have a child in a wheelchair.' I mean, this gradually grew and then after that we became prepared naturally.

The three oldest people with cerebral palsy were born in the late 1930s and the early 1940s and they drew particular attention to the fact that doctors in Ireland had little or no knowledge about cerebral palsy until the end of the 1940s. As a result, they were not actually diagnosed as having the condition until they were about seven or eight years old. This is how Christine described her mother's long search for a diagnosis and appropriate treatment throughout the 1940s:

When my mother did discover that there was something wrong, she brought me everywhere she could think of and nobody knew what cerebral palsy was and they didn't even know it existed. My mother started bringing me places from when I was about two years old. She really knew there was something wrong and no matter where she went they kept saying, 'Ah no, she's only a bit slow.' Eventually this doctor said to my mother that there was something wrong and he didn't know where he could advise her to take me. So in that time my mother just kept going. That went on for years. Mammy eventually found this doctor – he was English – and he started seeing us in his own house. He was the one that first said it was cerebral palsy.

Four of the ten people with multiple sclerosis said that they had not been told that they had the disease until quite a few years after the diagnosis had been made. Two of these, Eamonn and Helen, were grateful that their families and doctors had withheld the diagnosis from them and felt that they had been told about their condition at the right time. Eamonn, who had not become aware of his diagnosis until seventeen years after it had been made, summed up his perspective on this in the following way:

> The reason I was told in '72 was I got a very bad bout. I really thought I was on my last legs. Circumstances are the thing. It was best for me during those years that I didn't know because I would have used it as a kind of lever in reverse to say why I wasn't getting there. 'Ah sure, poor me. I have MS, sure you couldn't expect me to do it.' I was happy when I was told. You know what your potential, or whatever, is – physical, mental, the lot. So you can plan accordingly which is better in that you are building on a sound foundation. At least it mightn't be too sound but you're building on some kind of foundation.

9

In contrast, Carmel and Ger were bitter that they had not been told about their condition much earlier. Carmel said that her trust in her family and doctor had been undermined by their unwillingness, however well-meaning, to tell her the truth about her illness. Ger was bitter about the non-disclosure because she felt that it had prevented her from taking decisions which might have enabled her to slow down the progress of the disease:

> I wish they had told me thirteen years ago before I had the fourth child. They reckon that what dragged me down was having the baby.

All those whose diagnoses had been withheld from them – even if it was only for a short period – stressed that this caused enormous strain for anyone around them who *was* aware of the diagnosis. This tension was very much heightened if those with the disabling condition suspected that the truth was being kept from them and that they were in fact facing significant disability. Ger's husband was still uncertain about whether or not she should have been told from the beginning that she had multiple sclerosis and stressed that the years of trying to withhold the truth had been fraught with worry and tension:

> We talked about it meself and the doctor and we talked about the type of person she is. He thought to give her a shock would promote it more. In our wisdom, we said 'no', so that was it. And I spent up to five years ago saying, 'Ah, no, you haven't got it.' Even we'd be coming down the lift in the hospital and she'd have the card there and it was staring her in the face on the card. I could see it on the card but yet she couldn't see it. She couldn't see it. Like I knew she had it on her mind cos she was listening to the radio one morning and

they went through the whole thing, the way it affects you. The symptoms, each and every one of them, she had them. She was still trying to deny it to herself and she was trying to get me to confirm it and I was afraid to confirm it. When I did she went down mentally. She went as low as anyone could go. At the time, I think she went to death's door mentally.

Seven of those in the study felt that the disclosure of their diagnoses had been very poorly handled. Their main complaint was that the doctors and hospital personnel who were involved with them seemed to be ill-informed about their level of knowledge and also insensitive to the trauma of learning accidentally that one has a seriously disabling condition. Eddie, who had a spinal cord injury, talked angrily about the bungled way in which he had been told about the extent of his injuries shortly after he had been transferred from one hospital to another:

I was only there three days and on the third night the doctor comes up to me and says, 'You know you won't walk again?' I said, 'What are you talking about?' You know, I was sort of getting a bit together at this stage and I was after telling my mother to get all me shoes repaired and all to be ready for me when I'd come out – you see, not thinking. I didn't know, so how could I think? But he says, 'Ah no, you're paralysed from the neck down.' See, he had got the message wrong. He presumed the doctors had already told me but the doctors had already told my parents, not me. He thought I knew when I didn't. He walked off then anyway and that was it. Well, Jasus, that was it.

Kevin, who had suffered a spinal cord injury in the early 1960s, also felt that he had learned his prognosis in a very difficult way but attributed his bad experience to the fact that

11

the hospital where he was being treated was not used to dealing with people in his type of situation:

> The first time I found out it was so bad – this guy was visiting the hospital. There were no paraplegics in the hospital, just strokes and spastics. Next thing they brought this fella up to see me. 'Are you Kevin McNeill?' I said, 'Yeah.' 'I heard you had an accident the same as me,' he said. 'How long are you in that chair?' I asked him. 'I had the very same accident as you and I'm in a wheelchair fourteen years,' was his reply. I said, 'That's it. Don't bother askin' doctors or nothin'.' He was brought up to have a chat with me. He was after being in Stoke an' all. He was well used to the game. He must have thought I knew. When he came out with this I nearly passed out.

Quite a few of the people in the study said that they had asked either their doctors or members of their families to tell them exactly what was wrong soon after they first suspected that all was not well. All those who were told the truth at that stage were most appreciative that somebody had had the courage to be straight with them. Simon was among these and felt that his doctor's subsequent honesty had taken some of the harm out of his learning accidentally that he probably had multiple sclerosis:

> With me, I was lucky enough. I knew I had it when I was seventeen. Ah, the usual – double vision, into hospital. I read it on a chart while I was waiting to be seen by the doctor, 'Could be the early stages of multiple sclerosis.' So it took me aback. I enquired about it and, granted, me own doctor was straightforward. He said, 'Yeah, we can't be sure but we think you have it.' So after about six months the double vision cleared up and I didn't really think that much about it. Me own doctor advised me not to read up too much about

it. He sort of said, 'You'll start thinking things are happening to you before they actually happen.' It wasn't until four years later and they did a check-up that they told me, 'You definitely have it.' I was glad to know that I had it like and whenever I got these sensations I knew what it was.

Eoin, who was disabled as a result of a car crash, said that it had been extremely important to him that his brother had been prepared to answer his questions about the extent of his injuries and in doing so to show that he had faith in his ability to cope:

> My brother was dead straight with me. The hospital wouldn't tell me out straight. They told me brother, Tom, and he told me cos he knew I was a fighter kinda thing – no way I'd give in. He knew if he hadn'ta told me I probably would have bleedin' died, just lied back and died. I said to him, 'Look it, Tom, what's the scene here, what's happening?' Did they cut me bleedin' legs off or what?' He said to me, 'Eoin, they think you're paralysed and you mightn't walk again.' When I heard that I said to meself, there's no way I'm stayin' in this bed in this intensive care unit. I was only in that ICU for ten days and they couldn't believe it. They told me at the time that the only thing that saved me was me will and me build.

A number of those in the study made the point that the impressions which people receive when learning of their disabilities can significantly influence their early attitudes towards the prospect of having to live with disability for the rest of their lives. Eddie was particularly emphatic on this and described how he had seriously contemplated committing suicide in the weeks after he had been told of the extent of his injuries:

For three days and three nights I wouldn't eat, drink, sleep, nothing. I didn't want anybody near me or anything and they'd have to turn you and all this so that you wouldn't get pressure sores. I was just adamant that nobody would come near me. After three days and three nights of that I sort of said, 'Well, Jasus, what am I doing?' I sort of copped on. Not copped on as such but I said, 'I'm down, that's it. I'll just have to get back up.' I still couldn't sleep at nights. I don't know was it just the hospital – I'd say it was – the heat in the hospital and people snoring and moaning during the night and calling for nurses, this sort of thing. I ended up getting a sleeping tablet every night you see. So I started thinking to myself, 'Jasus, I'll keep these. I won't take them at all.' I gathered up a big load of them. And here I was, 'Jasus, this is grand. I'm going to do away with meself.' True to God for weeks I was storing them up. I just felt that I was a burden on everybody including me family. When they told me first they never said about what you can achieve for yourself in the end. They never turned around and said to me, 'You'll be able to dress yourself, wash yourself, feed yourself compared to somebody that's paralysed from the neck down.'

In contrast, Helen felt that the way in which she had learned that she had multiple sclerosis gave her a very positive view of her situation:

Paddy, my husband, knew for five years before I did. I started to get a bit bad then, more falls and everything. I don't know if you remember a programme that used to be on, *Positively Healthy*. Paddy rang me up this day from work and he said to me, 'Do you know the programme that we look at, *Positively Healthy*. It's on tonight and I think we should look at it.' And he came home and had his dinner and we went in and looked at the television and there was a doctor on it and a few people that had MS and they were all giving their symptoms of how it started, what happened to them and each one of them that said something I was saying to myself, 'I have it, that's what I have.' I don't think I ever heard tell of MS up to that point. By the end of the programme I knew what I had and I said to Paddy, 'That's what I have, isn't it?' So he just said, 'Yes.' I asked him how long had I got it and he said, 'Five years.' The way I heard it, it was beautiful because I was looking at happy people and they were having a joke and a laugh about it, saying, 'Yes, okay, we were shocked when we were told. It was awful.' One person said, I think, 'It was like being run over by a car and being able to stand up again sort of thing.'

Summary

It is probably true to say that most people in our society see disability as a fact of life and it is certainly not uncommon for people to become disabled. It is not so easy to make generalisations about the individual experience of becoming disabled because everyone's situation is unique. Even people with the same disabling condition can be affected in very different ways.

It was striking that almost everyone in the study stressed that they had been very ignorant about disability until it had entered their own lives. They did not see themselves as being unusual in this regard and pointed to the ongoing ignorance about disability among the ablebodied population in Ireland.

The experience of learning one's diagnosis is a crucial turning point in the life of each individual with a disabling condition. It emerged from the interviews as one which is carved into the memory and unlikely ever to be forgotten. The clear message which rings out from the experiences of the people in this study is that it matters greatly how the whole issue of disclosure is handled. What they saw as important was to be told sensitively by someone they felt they could trust, and in a manner which let them see that they still had many abilities left to them.

Chapter 2

What can be done for me?

Anyone in Ireland who has a physically disabling condition will almost certainly have had a good deal of contact with the world of medicine and the wide range of professionals who are associated with it. This was true of all the people in the study and their specific experiences were determined largely by their diagnoses and by the time in history when they first became disabled. In many respects it seemed that, once a final diagnosis had been made, a fairly standard road of treatment was opened up to 'patients' affected by a particular disabling condition. We will look firstly at the experiences of the people with cerebral palsy and then turn to the experiences of the people with spinal cord injuries and multiple sclerosis.

'This might work, this might not work'

The four oldest people with cerebral palsy were those who had experienced the most prolonged periods of hospitalisation. All these had been in orthopaedic hospitals for four to five years when they were young, having a series of operations which were aimed at improving their level of mobility. Peter, who was born in 1942, stressed that the treatment which he had received had been experimental, time-consuming and ultimately ineffective:

> Anyway, 1947 came around and I ended up in an orthopaedic hospital. My surgeon operated. I think he was hitting and missing, you know what I mean? He did something to my stomach which loosened a few muscles and made the limbs more flexible and I ended up in steels and crutches after foot operations and stomach operations. So I was on crutches feckin' around in hospital 'til 1952. Actually, I left the hospital walking on crutches and steels but due to a mixture of laziness and not being part of having to prove anything I got lazy again. I had to have more operations. They were racing against time before I became twenty-one. After twenty-one, it would be no use doing anything, you know what I mean? But even at that, after twenty-one, right up to me thirties, I had operations on the foot to try and keep it straight. But my surgeon, never the most optimistic of men, quite rightly too, said, 'This might work, this might not work.'

Brian, who was in an orthopaedic hospital for six years from the age of three, said that he had been reasonably happy there but had gained little or nothing from the whole experience:

> The reason for going into hospital was to see could they do anything for me like straighten out my legs and the doctors six years later discovered it was impossible. I liked it there. I looked forward to seeing Mummy and Daddy once a week and I suppose the nurses were as kind as they could be. My biggest memory like is that outside of the hospital I thought the world was out there, America, Australia and all. I had no perception of what the outside world was. I seen my brother twice in six years and I always heard my mother telling me

that my Daddy worked. I thought by working she meant that he dug the garden or that he worked in the house. So I was totally disorientated towards outside society and when I came out of Cappagh I found it hard to believe that if you go down the road you are still in one locality.

Christine described her life as having been dominated by lengthy stays in hospital from the time she was six years old. She had numerous operations over a period of about twenty years which were aimed at enabling her to walk independently. It was not until she was twenty-eight that this dream was realised and she experienced a few years of 'freedom' before becoming affected by arthritis:

Before the operation, it used to be if Mammy couldn't go then I couldn't go. But then when I got the crutches it meant a new life to me in a sense because I discovered one thing and that was that I could cross the road on my own, a thing I hadn't done in all my life. I discovered that I could get up and down steps and across roads and stand in the middle of the road if I wanted to. It was a whole new experience for me to be able to jump on a bus on my own. I began to do things on my own and I began to make friends and meet people. I even started going to dances. I feel now that Mammy was right, that I'd had one or two operations too many which meant that I got arthritis quicker than I would have if I had left well alone. But I think, honestly speaking, if it meant that I never walked, I still had to try that. I wouldn't have been happy unless I tried. I think if I thought there was a chance, even the slightest chance, of me being able to get up and walk around again – even a little bit – I'd take that chance. I'd never let a thing like that pass me by. I'd always have to say, 'Well now I tried.' I'd always do that.

The practice of treating children with cerebral palsy in orthopaedic hospitals over very lengthy periods began to decline from the mid-1950s onwards. This was due in large part to the establishment of out-patient clinics which provided many of the services, such as physiotherapy and speech therapy, which had previously been available only to the patients of orthopaedic hospitals. The early clinics were very basic and parents often had to undergo considerable hardship in the pursuit of treatment for their children. Brian's mother recalled the years when she brought him across Dublin each morning for physiotherapy:

> I used to attend a place every morning for three years. Every morning I used to have to sit in a park reading a book while he got half an hour's physiotherapy. Like they used to have bricks and different things to work the fingers. But every morning I had to go. You couldn't get in to sit with them.

The younger people with cerebral palsy did not undergo anything like as much surgery as their older counterparts. Most had had just one operation while the core of their treatment was regular physiotherapy, usually until their late teens. The parents of the younger people certainly had greater medical expertise and better services available to them than the parents of those who were born in the early 1940s. However, they also had to work hard to ensure that their children received the treatment which they needed. Paul, who was born in 1957, was the youngest person with cerebral palsy and his mother recalled the difficulties and stresses which were involved when he first began having regular physiotherapy:

> So when he was coming up to three, I approached a spastic

specialist to see if anything could be done for him. At this stage I was expecting my second child. I had to take him on two buses a couple of days a week for physiotherapy. Eventually, when I couldn't carry him, I went to my own doctor and he gave me a letter for the specialist and without even opening the letter she said that he would be collected every day. He went then for physiotherapy every second day or so. The transport in those days was awful and there wasn't enough for all the kids they had to take. And they had to depend on voluntary drivers which meant that Paul could be sitting in that window day after day and maybe not get a lift. But things have eased up since then. But it was awful because I had no car then. We had no car at all and there was no way of getting him there. And with handicapped children, if you tell them you are going to call they don't think that you are telling lies. They think you are going to call, do you understand? I've often said to Paul, 'Don't take people at their word. They don't really mean it.' But he would think, 'They said they'd call. Why don't they call?'

The parents of two of the younger people with cerebral palsy extended their search for treatment for their children beyond the confines of the developing services in Ireland and sought help in England. Jane underwent surgery at a London hospital when she was sixteen years old and stayed there for approximately two months to follow a rehabilitation programme. Jane herself was not particularly enthusiastic about the outcome of the operation as she felt that it had not helped her mobility to any significant extent. Her mother, on the other hand, had been very pleased with the results of the surgery and stressed that it had improved her appearance greatly:

Like, the improvement was only so fantastic like it wasn't true. Jane was completely cross-legged and she couldn't sit properly so if she hadn't gone she'd have looked absolutely diabolical. I mean, it made her into somebody that could do something for herself. She can really do nothing for herself but it made her that she could be accepted and before she was in such a disastrous state. She was getting heavier and they wouldn't do the operation here. No doctor would. They wouldn't even give her a letter to go to London. They said that nothing could be done for her and that this was a mental thing which of course it is. She's lucky that she was left with intelligence – you know that that wasn't blocked. They said on account of this that nothing could be done. But immediately the doctor saw her in London, he said, 'Oh yes, I can straighten out her legs,' and he had to do a big job on her groin that she would be able to sit properly.

Billy was the other person who was brought to England in search of treatment. His mother explained that she had found it very difficult to get information about cerebral palsy in Ireland and that she had been utterly determined to ensure that her son was given the best treatment possible:

I suppose some people are happy to just go along but I'm not. I felt there was a dearth of information. I was talking to his physiotherapist one day and I said, 'I wonder is there anything we can do?' She said, 'If you think of taking him to London, I know a physiotherapist there and I'll write to her.' She wrote to her and she told me that there was a doctor in Harley Street who would be worth taking him to. This all sounds as if we had loads of money – we didn't actually at all. And now he has a medical card for years but at that time if he had polio everything was paid for because it was an infectious disease but as he didn't have an infectious disease we had to pay for his physiotherapy and everything.

At this stage, we had four children and not too much money, you know the way it is. You feel you would scrub floors if necessary and everything worked out so well. The visit to Doctor Black in London was very successful. I went along with a sheaf of questions and he sat there for an hour answering my questions while I wrote down the answers. In the end, he said that there wasn't anything more that he could advise. We were going on the right lines, had the right ideas and so on. He put us in touch with a doctor in Dublin who he had worked with and he said that he would be aware of all the latest developments as they came out.

There was quite a degree of tension between the parents of three of those with cerebral palsy over their disability and the matter of pursuing treatment for it. Brian's mother, for example, said that she and her husband had disagreed over whether or not he should be placed in residential care when he was nine years old, having just spent six years in hospital undergoing different forms of treatment. She wanted to keep him at home and managed to do this but felt that it was very much in spite of her husband's wishes:

> He was on the list for John of God's. They had a batch going out to John of God's, into a home like, but I wouldn't let him go. Me GP told me he'd never be any good – he wouldn't make any progress and that it would be best if I let him go to John of God's. When I told me husband that he was listed for John of God's, he said, 'Maybe it would be better if we let him go. What can we do for him?' I got his clothes ready for him that night and I put his clothes in the go-car the next morning and went off to the hospital to collect him. I had Brian home and all before me husband came home. I said, 'He's not going to John of God's,' and he more or less put it, 'You're after takin' him out so you look after him.'

Christine's parents separated when she was thirteen years old after years of quarrelling and tension which was often associated with her disability:

> My father never understood that my mother had to bring me to the clinic everyday. His dinner had to be on the table like when he came in so she'd be breaking her neck getting home. She was worried then if she was late, you know, cos there'd be a row over it. There used to be rows every night and if my mother wanted to bring me with her when we'd be going out he wouldn't want to go. I used to hear a lot of arguments but didn't understand them until I got a lot older and then I began to realise that I was the cause of them. He always blamed my mother for my disability and not himself. He never accepted me.

All those with cerebral palsy said that the search for treatment, which had in some cases almost completely dominated their earlier years, was now very much a part of the past. It was clear that their hopes of securing any significant improvements had long since faded. Most, like Jane, stressed that the costs associated with undergoing any further treatment would far outweigh the benefits which might be derived from doing this:

> They always hoped up 'til the time I was eighteen that I'd walk. It was always sort of there. Before the operation, they thought that if I did have one that it might sort of help me walk or that. Okay, it helped me that I could straighten my legs. I was very bent before that. Now they are straight when I stand up but I myself felt that there was no more point to treatment if I was going to work and that. I wasn't going to get any worse by not having it which I haven't. I myself felt it was a waste of time. You know it would be. Certainly, having to get off work and to have to go to physiotherapy cos it wouldn't really be doing me any good any more.

Regular medical attention is by no means a feature of the lives of all adults with cerebral palsy. Nine of the ten in the study said that their general health was good and that they had little or no contact now with doctors or other health care professionals. Brian was one of these:

I don't have any illnesses that are either related or not related to my cerebral palsy. Thank God, I have no side disabilities. The only disability that I have is cerebral palsy. In earlier years when I came out of hospital – up to the age of about seventeen or eighteen – I used to take turns like. I would go into a fit which would last for about three or four minutes and immediately after that I wouldn't be able to talk. I'd feel it about three days before it actually came. I mean, I could tell my mother or father that I was going to have a fit and I would take the necessary precautions but they died out altogether after I think – ah God – eighteen.

In contrast, Christine, who at forty-four was one of the oldest people with cerebral palsy, said that she suffered from a whole series of physical problems which required ongoing medical attention. These included rheumatoid arthritis and stress incontinence which, combined, had reduced her interest in going out as much as she had previously:

I'll be honest. I have to take the fluid tablets and they keep working from around tea-time until midnight. I go to bed at twelve and I'm up at seven. See, if I take them in the morning I couldn't go to work. And then I've got what they call stress incontinence since I had the hysterectomy. So it's not on to go out. If I go out, especially at the moment – see, me legs are paining me all the time. The only ease I get is when I get into bed.

'The price of function is eternal vigilance'

Sustaining a spinal cord injury in Ireland almost always means being admitted to the National Spinal Injuries Unit in Dublin for a lengthy period of rehabilitation. The length of stay for the ten people in the study ranged from eight months to over two and a half years with most being there for almost a year and a half. For this group then, the first direct experiences of learning to live with disability and face the future take place away from familiar home surroundings and among other people going through something very similar.

Accidents serious enough to cause spinal cord injuries often result in a number of other major physical problems which can lead to serious complications in the immediate post-injury period and it can take many weeks or months before a reasonable degree of stability is achieved in the patient's overall condition. In Conor's case, for example, it was not until six or seven months after he had been struck by a car that he eventually came out of intensive care:

> For the first six, seven, eight months I was still critical all the time. Apparently one of my lungs collapsed. I was in ICU for January, February, March, April and then I was brought into the big ward. Then I was back in the cubicle. The cubicle is something like a semi-ICU. This was going on for at least seven months. They had to fix up the lung first before they knew what the injury was and then they came across the spinal injury.

One of the main features about the rehabilitation experience of people with spinal cord injury is that they face the paradoxical situation of realising that they have lost a significant degree of physical function at a time when they are experiencing a considerable improvement in their condition. For Paddy, this was one of the most notable aspects of his time in the rehabilitation centre:

> The first time it hit me was the first time I was told to get into a wheelchair. See, you're lying on a bed for so long and then you're allowed to sit up for so long each day. Like, you're in Intensive Care first and then you're shifted out into the ward. When you're shifted out you're still in Intensive Care sort of thing but you're in a main ward. You're fit enough to put up with the rest of them. I remember, yeh, I think that was the greatest shock I got, when I sat into the wheelchair. I thought, 'There's more wrong here than...'
>
> See, before you're in bed so long you assume you can walk. Nothing had registered with me before that. When you were taken out of bed, you were allowed in the wheelchair, I think it's for about four minutes before you turn as white as a sheet because you've been lying down so long. So then the next day it's extended time-wise, maybe twenty minutes, then thirty minutes, then they might leave you out for an hour every day until you got used to sitting up in a chair. And then there was OT. The greatest shock of the whole lot was when you know this thing is not going to last just so long – just a fortnight or whatever.

Physiotherapy is the main form of treatment for people who have suffered a spinal cord injury and most of the people in the study stressed that they had worked really hard at this. Some, like Eddie who had contemplated suicide at one point after learning about the extent of his injuries, said that they had thrown themselves into the physiotherapy as they felt that it was the one way they could actively contribute towards helping themselves:

I was always outgoing sort of – going to parties, twenty-firsts, going somewhere. You know, somewhere different all the time. Then, there you are stuck in hospital all of a sudden. So I decided, 'This is it, the tablets.' I said, 'That's it, I'm going to start taking them.' But I didn't. I just went to the loo and flushed them down. I don't know why. To this day, I don't know why I didn't take them. Flushed them all away and I said, 'I'm going to get out of this place. I don't care how or in what state. I'm just going to get out of this place.' So I started going down to physiotherapy again next day and, Jesus, I worked like a nigger. The sweat was pumping out of me. I wouldn't leave the place.

All stressed that they had eventually got into a familiar daily routine during their long stay at the rehabilitation centre and that this had helped to pass the time. Kevin, who had his accident in the early 1960s, said that the hospital regime was very strict during his time there but that he and some of the other patients had found ways around the rules, especially those associated with going out at night:

> The hospital was very regimental. You couldn't breathe. The nuns were very strict that time. To go out for a pint at night you used to have to wait until they said their few prayers at six o'clock and then we'd sneak out the back way. We often used to have to cross two fields and out a side gate to get down for a pint. And there'd be murder. They'd come down to the pub an' all after you and order you out. They were very narrow-minded that time. Say you went for a ramble round the place and started talking to one of the staff, that broke every rule in the book. There was no patients and staff mixing. It's very lax out there now. Now when they *can* go out, they often don't bother going.

Hugh, who was in the rehabilitation centre around 1980, described the timetable as being very structured but the atmosphere and staff/patient interaction as being much more relaxed than some twenty years earlier:

> The toughest part for me was being confined to bed for the first sixteen weeks and that was tough. The day seemed very long. After you get out of bed, then it's mainly physiotherapy and stuff like that. Then it becomes nearly like a nine-to-five job. You get up in the morning, you go down to physio, then you have occupational therapy in the afternoon. You're finished at about five. In fact, you can go out at night time from the hospital. I think, to be honest with you, it's all part of the rehab or whatever, getting used to going out in the chair. Me father might come up or Mary might come up and we'd go down to the local, about half a mile away. It got you used to being out in public in the chair. You didn't even realise it. You look on it as a treat to get out. You don't think, 'I'm going out in me chair.' You just think, 'I'm getting out.'
>
> You know, you spend so long in there it's fantastic to get out. It works great that way. You're not just thrown in at the deep end. The hospital is really fantastic; the nurses are fantastic. The nurses aren't like nurses. The nurses were at the stage where with the lads from down the country, they'd say, 'I'll be back to you at eight o'clock and we'll go out and have a drink,' and they'd bring guys out to the pub. They kinda worked outside their hours. They were great like that.

It was clear that the formal treatment provided in the hospital was only part of the overall experience. All ten stressed the positive effects which they had derived from interacting with the other patients in the Spinal Injury Unit. The camaraderie amongst the patients was highlighted and there was a general consensus that, irrespective of one's own condition, the hospital unfailingly provided the opportunity of regular contact with patients who seemed even less fortunate. This was identified by each as having contributed greatly towards reducing their own self-pity. All stressed that there was little or no tolerance among either staff or patients for individuals who were perceived as being self-pitying. As Conor explained:

> When you're in hospital and you've crowds of people around you, you've no time to feel sorry for yourself. If you feel sorry for yourself, you're out, you're not accepted. What keeps most of them going is you always see someone worse than yourself – like, no matter how bad you are, you'll always see someone ten times worse. The first thing a nurse would say to you, 'What's wrong with you? Look at that poor chap up there.' That takes the wind out of your sails straightaway. I think the older people are, the harder it is for them. When you're younger you seem to be able to get on with it – if they're older when it happens first, they realise on the spot what's wrong with them where the other gombeen doesn't until it's too late. He's out of the bed and down in the gym an' all before he realises the brief.

Most of the people in the study had been home for a number of weekends prior to being discharged fully from the Spinal Injuries Unit. All these felt that this had helped them to make a break from the security of the hospital and get an idea of what it would be like to be living again in the outside world. Eddie, for example, stressed that visiting home had made him extremely aware of the whole problem of wheelchair access:

> I went home for the Christmas Day after me accident in June. That was me first time being home. The house looked really

small after being in the hospital with tons of room, corridors miles wide. It was only when you come home that you realise that the wheelchair is like an armchair in the house.

Making the final break from the Spinal Injuries Unit was considered to be a very significant stepping stone along the path of rehabilitation. However, as Paddy observed, it was also a highly emotional time:

People used to cry leaving there cos it's classed as a family unit sort of thing. We got to know each other so personally. Like, you were so long in the place. You were so long together that when it came to time to go I've seen fellas crying leaving the place. The brothers, say, may work in Dublin and sometimes they'd drop them back up to the hospital again just to meet those who were left.

Eoin pointed out that it was very hard to go from being one of the strongest in the hospital and a person who could 'do push-ups with a physiotherapist sitting on me back' to being a weakling in the 'outside world'. For him, the day of his final discharge from hospital was a much feared, low point in his career:

It bothered me comin' out of hospital. I didn't want to come out of hospital. Like, coming home and seeing your friends and neighbours – like, these were people that didn't mind, they understood. But I didn't understand. Me brother gave me a lift home in the car. I had to get lifted out of the car and get lifted into the car and at the beginning as well I had to get lifted into bed; I had to get lifted out of bed; I had to get dressed. Everything had to get done for me but I can do everything now for meself. I'm in the wheelchair eight years. If I hadn't learned anything in eight years I might as well go into the 'Glas' (graveyard) and bury meself alive.

It was clear that everyone was keenly aware of the dangers surrounding the medical complications which can be associated with spinal cord injury. Nine of the ten said that they returned to hospital for annual check-ups and there was a general consensus that, as Dolores put it, 'the price of function is eternal vigilance'. The eight whose lesions were incomplete highlighted their fortunate positions compared with those with complete lesions in relation to the development of complications such as pressure sores and urinary infections. Hugh, for example, commented:

> The bladder is the main problem when you're disabled. You can have a lot of problems. The bladder is very lazy and you get infections. They can be serious but with me they're not. I know when I have an infection. A lot of people get infections when they're badly disabled and they don't know they have it and the next thing they'll end up conked out in a bad way, whereas I can tell when I have one and go down to the doctor and get a course of tablets and in a few days it's gone. I'm lucky that way. The other problem you can have in a wheelchair is pressure sores. Again, I don't get them because I'm not a complete paraplegic. I'm one of the better off as regards disability. There's a lot worse off than me.

However, all ten had experienced complications at some point and there were five cases in which these had been particularly severe. Gerry, for example, described how he had suffered for about four years as a result of a 'tumble':

> I fell on my ass and cut it and rule number one in this game is never damage your ass because it's more important than your head. You have to sit on it all day and it's extremely delicate. There's no way round it, you have to sit on it. I developed a sort of a growth. I took advice and three

surgeons said, 'Yes', and three surgeons said, 'No, don't go near it for the simple reason that you can't predict the outcome.' This was an extremely delicate choice to have to make but it was a life-orienting choice in the sense that to get about and generally enjoy life you have to sit on your ass but the more you sat on it the more angry and inflamed it became. This is where, ironically, my levels of sensation both served me and hurt me. Because where the normal paraplegic or quadriplegic could sit on that all day and not feel it, I can. So, four operations later the thing was sorted out. I lost three and a half, nearly four years, feckin' around with that.

All ten talked at some length about their approach towards the issue of being cured. It seemed that each of them had sustained at least some hope of being fully cured even after they had been told about the extent of their injuries. These hopes had been heightened with the return of even very limited movement. However, in eight cases they had been eroded completely with the passing of time. Al described this fading of hope in the following way:

> The family and the injured person tend to think in the very short term. They look for a restoration of what was before, and even if after – in my own case – eleven months you can move a finger you say, 'Jasus, if I can move that finger in eleven months, in another eleven months all the fingers will be back and we'll start working on the legs.' It takes maybe three, four, five years to realise that they're not going to work, that your dancing days are done.

Hugh pointed out that, even though he himself had lost all hope of being cured shortly after his accident eight years earlier, it was only now that one of his young sons was beginning to accept that his dad would never walk again:

The youngest fella never knew me out of the chair. The older one was only two but he still remembers. And all the photographs with his Daddy, you know. It really played on his mind last summer and he thought I was going to get better and be able to bring him off and play football. But he's not so bad now. A few weeks ago, I was in the kitchen and he said, 'Daddy, I don't think you're going to get better, sure you're not?' And I said, 'No son, I'm not. I'll be like this always.' And he mentioned some of the things I *can* do and let it go at that. I think he's beginning to accept it. The little fella, it doesn't bother him at all. He couldn't care less.

Both Dolores and Eoin said that the hope of cure was still important to them even after being disabled for twenty-one and eight years respectively. Each defined their continued hope as a manifestation of their general determination on which they really prided themselves. This was how Dolores described her feelings:

I always think they might find something. Even if I was forty or forty something, I'd be saying maybe I could get something done. At the same time, you kind of accept the chair, that you're in it until they do. And if your health is good enough when it does come there's always a chance you could get something done. You get used to it; it's part of you – the chair – you know. But you're still always hoping, with me anyway, that there's a chance you might get out of it. I do anyway. I don't know what other people think. Maybe some people give up but I'm not a one that gives up easily. I'll fight a thing to the end.

'Mum, you were born fifty years too early'

There are few certainties associated with multiple sclerosis but one of these is that the cure for the disease remains unknown. The treatment which tends to be offered by orthodox medicine is centred around drug therapy and all the people in this study were on at least one form of medication for their condition. Some, like Ger, stressed that they had been helped greatly by some of the drugs which were prescribed for them:

> They tried all sorts of medicines on me to see what I would react to best. Then I went on cortisone and that brought me up fantastic but I put on two and a half stone weight. I was on cortisone for five years. I was able to do all me housework. But they had to take me off the cortisone after five years because it affects the bones in the back or something. They can't put me on that again. I do some of me housework still. I'm able to get around but me balance is gone. I'm on Immuran now for the last three years and that's the best thing that ever happened. Depression is dreadful with me. Depression is the worst, although I'm on depression tablets all the time. It's very bad now at the moment. I never suffered with depression before I got MS. I was always a happy-go-lucky person – always running. I never walked. I always used to thank God that I was able, which is amazing how it used to always go through my mind.

Deirdre, on the other hand, stressed that her life was almost intolerable in spite of having tried all sorts of different medications to alleviate the 'spasms' which had developed in her legs:

It's a kind of crampy pain; you can't move your legs. Am I depressing you just talking about it? I was always independent that I could do things meself even though I had MS. It's only lately now since I got these spasms I can't do anything. As I said I was resigned to the MS. I had it and that was it and I knew there was no cure for it but, Jesus, these spasms. I used to say I wouldn't let MS beat me but these spasms, they have me bet. They'd wake you if you were dead. I don't think there's much they can do with them only try you on different tablets. As you know, there's no cure for multiple sclerosis. I'm on the strongest painkillers; I'm on loads of tablets. Will I show you all the tablets I'm on? They've tried everything with me. Now last night, it was so bad I was roaring and crying in the bed. I was hoping God would take me but it mustn't be me time.

Most people had attended physiotherapy sessions at some stage to work on their mobility. There were mixed views on the benefits of this. Simon, who was in residential care, was adamant that physiotherapy and exercise was very helpful in his particular case:

There is a physiotherapist comes in here twice a week but you only see her for about three minutes. That's not enough so I do me own thing. There are parallel bars and I do various exercises like weights. If I don't exercise, I feel very tired. I used to walk in the garden and one time a nurse here, she said to me during a relapse, 'You won't walk in the garden again.' I said, 'You had better go back and get a refresher course in MS.' I said, 'You haven't got a clue about it; it hits everybody differently, in a unique way.' I said, 'You are generalising,' I said, 'and you don't generalise with MS.' Two weeks later I was back in the garden exercising.

Debbie, who had been attending physiotherapy privately for about three years, was less sure about its physical benefits but felt that it was good for her morale:

> At the physio, they are all very helpful. It's only to see if this leg is working enough. It doesn't change at all. I don't think it does me very much good but it's good, I think, that I have to go every week, to drive there, drive properly and observe everything and get there and come back. I often go into someone on the way home or someone is coming here at eleven so I have to hurry up and come home.

Hospitalisation did not feature very much in the lives of those with multiple sclerosis especially when compared to those with spinal injury or, indeed, cerebral palsy. However, everyone had been in hospital at some point in connection with the disease. Three had had operations to alleviate bladder complaints. Elaine was one of these and she described how she had actively pursued surgery which she felt might help her incontinence problem:

> I got it into me head through a cousin in America. She has a friend also with MS and she has this bladder trouble. So she was taken into hospital for ten days and they cured the bladder trouble. So I went up to my doctor and said, 'Look, I want that. When she could get it done in America, we have as good a doctor in Ireland as was ever in America.' 'Right,' says he, 'But I don't agree.' 'Well', says I, 'get me to someone.' So he sent me to another man and he said, 'I don't think I can get anyone to do it.' 'Ah, look', says I, 'for God's sake, what are you talking about?' So he got this surgeon and I went and had the operation. But no success. 'I told you,' said he, 'I told you but you were adamant about it because of your cousin in America.'

But I tried and I was happy once I tried and I had three operations while I was there. They were getting that fed up with me, it was a case of, 'When in the name of God are you going home?' There was a dark doctor came in one day and he had a cure for it. My own surgeon was there and he said, 'Don't mention operation to her cos she'll say yes.'

There were very mixed views about the experience of being hospitalised alongside other people with multiple sclerosis. Eamonn said that it had done him good in that he had become friendly with another person with the disease and had begun to feel relatively fortunate:

The greatest lesson I ever learned was going into hospital in 1972. I had to be brought in in the ambulance. I couldn't urinate and had to be brought down to theatre. What was good for me was the psychological rather than the physical. The physical did me good too but when you go into hospital you see people that are worse than yourself. Now generally these people aren't people that are complaining. They are the best characters in the place; they uplift everybody. And you realise and you say to yourself, 'What kind of a bloody eejit are you, complaining. Look at that fella.' The man in the bed beside me had MS and he was a great guy too. He is one of these people who would never let it beat him and I think you have to fight. Now he'd still ring up every so often or write to me and say, 'There's a new drug out that's going to cure you,' or, 'You shouldn't be eating apples' or something.

Ger, on the other hand, reacted very badly to being in a ward which catered mainly for people with multiple sclerosis and her husband stressed that he would do his utmost to keep her at home if he possibly could:

The last time she came out of hospital, she came out totally worse than she went in, just seeing the other people suffering from the same disease in different stages. Some of them were in these rotary beds. She was actually shattered and the only way I could get her out was I agreed to a home help. I would have agreed to shoot somebody at the time to get her out. I said, 'Never again.' No matter what state she goes into because of her complaint, as long as we can keep her here at home, she'll never go into that atmosphere again. It doesn't do her any good. There is really no point. There is nothing they can do. We can do more here as a family for one another than any hospital can do. The rest in hospital possibly might have done her good if she had been in another ward than the ward she was in – the multiple sclerosis ward – realising that that's what's in front of her.

All ten people with multiple sclerosis were patients of both a neurologist and a general practitioner. They tended to see their neurologists about twice each year and most were in contact with their general practitioners on a monthly or more regular basis. Indeed, four of the ten said that their general practitioners were extremely helpful to them and were very significant people in their lives. Carmel was among these:

I do have the doctor down two or three times a week to give me an injection. He's very good. I don't know what I'd do without him. He is really a friend to the family.

At the other extreme, Deirdre and Anne were very dissatisfied with their general practitioners. They felt that the doctors had only very limited knowledge about MS and that they had a tendency to refer them needlessly to their neurologists. Thus, according to Anne:

Me GP does be afraid I'm going to die on his hands. 'You'd better get down and see Dr Byrne.' And I say to Dr Byrne, 'That's why I'm here, me GP said I'd better come down and see you. Only for that I wouldn't come near you but I think when he sees me he thinks I'm going to die.' So he says, 'You're not going to die yet for another few years. Come back in a year or two's time.' 'Unless you find something that cures me,' says I, 'you get in touch with me.'

Everyone was very aware of the range of purported 'cures' for MS and most had tried at least one of them. However, none felt that they had benefited from these and Helen, for example, pointed out that her willingness to try 'cures' had led to both physical and financial suffering:

If I thought a decompression chamber would do any good, I'd buy one for meself. I'd never come out of it, I can tell you, if I thought it would make me well. Ah, Jesus, I tried all sorts of cures. That fella in the Park Hotel. Fair play, he prayed over me and I could see meself walking out of the place but I didn't. And I tried a diet. Don't talk to me about it. It nearly killed me. My husband, he went down and he must have spent £50 which we hadn't got: made a collection around the whole lot of the family. Fifty pound he spent on buying certain kinds of flour, soya beans, you know, instead of your meat. I lost weight and I never got it back. I tried it for a month.

There was a general feeling that a cure for MS would eventually be found and Carmel, in particular, talked of how she yearned to hear of a break-through in research on the disease:

I love the news and I do often say to Mammy that maybe a flash would come up to say they've found a cure for MS.

Debbie, like most of the others, felt that even if a cure was found it could only prevent a worsening of her condition and not bring back what had already been lost:

> I often think why the dickens does it have to be me. I can think of people who would love to be sitting in a wheelchair all day – people who don't want to do as much physically. It's a sort of lovely, lazy existence, you might think, but I've always loved to *do* things. See, there is no reason why it gets to you. It's so undiscovered. Our son said to me, 'Mum, you were born fifty years too early.' I will never get better if they discover a pill to take tomorrow but I would never get any worse. I suppose medically it's a shrivelling of the nerve endings. See, you don't feel. It's your nerve endings that are wrong. They would never come back.

Summary

It would be most unusual for anyone in Ireland with a physically disabling condition like cerebral palsy, multiple sclerosis or spinal cord injury not to have at least some contact with medical and paramedical personnel. It was not surprising, then, to find that all thirty people in the study had looked to medicine for treatment for their conditions. The type of treatment they received varied depending on the nature of their condition and the point in history when they sought it. The most notable change over the years was that it became much less common for children with cerebral palsy to spend prolonged periods in orthopaedic hospitals having various operations and other forms of treatment.

The treatment received by those with spinal cord injuries was much more standardised than that of those with either cerebral palsy or multiple sclerosis. Everyone with a spinal cord injury spent at least eight months in a rehabilitation centre following their accidents. In contrast, none of those with multiple sclerosis spent prolonged periods in hospital and their treatment consisted mainly of drug therapy aimed at controlling their often wide-ranging and varied symptoms.

A few of those interviewed said that they held out some hopes of being 'cured'. These were people with multiple sclerosis and spinal cord injuries – acquired conditions in which the sense of loss and the longing to regain former abilities can be very strong.

CHAPTER 3

EDUCATION

In Ireland, going to school, and perhaps on to college or
university, is one of the most taken-for-granted aspects of
growing up. Children's lives tend to revolve around the
school year and a child's age generally translates neatly into a
particular stage in the educational process. But what about
people with physical disabilities? What is the educational
system like from their perspectives and what experiences
have they had? Also, how do those who have acquired their
disabilities in adult life feel about their education and
qualifications in the light of how their lives have turned out?
This chapter will seek to answer these questions. It will focus
firstly on those who have experienced the educational system
as people with disabilities and then broaden out to include
those who acquired their disabilities after they had
completed their formal education.

Thirteen of the people in the study had direct
experience of the educational system as people with
disabilities. These included all ten with cerebral palsy. They
also included Gerry who was injured in a car crash and
Eamonn and Simon who had MS. These last three were well
advanced in their education before becoming disabled and

their experience of the system as people with disabilities was restricted to that at third level.

The period in which these thirteen were involved in education extended from the mid-1940s to the mid-1970s. This was a time in which there were many developments in relation to educational provision for people with physical disabilities in Ireland. In short, these decades saw a shift away from segregated education in residential hospital schools and special day schools in favour of a more integrated approach in which pupils with physical disabilities are provided with special facilities to enable them to attend ordinary school. This broad pattern of development is very much reflected in the educational history of the group as a whole.

'Take your hand off the bannisters or you'll take the shine off them'

Christine and Paula were the only two with cerebral palsy who had attended ordinary primary schools. They were both born in 1939 and were the oldest of this group. They stressed that ordinary school was all that was available to them in the mid-1940s because special day schools had not yet been established and their parents did not want to have them placed in long-stay hospitals where they could have attended classes. Neither had satisfactory experiences at the primary schools they attended and both left prematurely because of what they described as the inflexibility and lack of understanding shown by the school authorities. Christine had vivid memories of this time:

Mammy couldn't get any school in Dublin to take me. They wouldn't take a handicapped person. Then she got me into one and she used to have to wheel me there and wheel me back. I was there for two years but, you see, third class was upstairs and I remember the nun saying to me and I holding the bannisters going up the stairs, 'Take your hand off the bannisters or you'll take the shine off them.' I used to get a terrible lot of chilblains and things like that and the doctor said I was to wear trousers, you know, warm stockings and all this type of thing. And I remember my mother; it took her six months to save the money to be able to buy me these things that the doctor suggested that I should wear. We had no medical cards at that time.

The next thing, anyway, this nun comes in and she called me out of the class. I used to have two sticks, so I went out and she said, 'Go home and take those trousers and shoes and stockings off you and come back decently dressed.' It was a uniform we wore. I said, 'But the doctor said I was to wear them.' 'No way', she said. 'Go home right now.' 'I can't,' I said, 'because Mammy has to collect me.' Anyway, my mother took me out of it and that was the end of it. I never went back.

'School only provided a source of occupation'

Both Peter and Brian had experience of hospital schools. They had gained this during stays of up to five or six years in orthopaedic hospitals when they were aged between three and ten years. Both stressed that the standard of education which they received in these classes was very low. Thus, according to Brian:

School only provided a source of occupation, sort of something to do for two or three hours per day. It bore no resemblance whatever to the academic aspect of education.

Some of the parents of those with cerebral palsy stressed that they had been extremely concerned about the disruption which was caused to their chidren's education by the need for medical treatment or by the difficulties associated with getting them accepted into school in the first place. These parents recalled how they had felt that a good education was even more essential for their children than for non-disabled children but how, at the same time, they had been acutely aware of the fact that children with disabilities face far more difficulties than normal children in securing high quality schooling. Both Jane and Billy's parents decided to get a private tutor for them when they were very young as they felt that this would compensate for some of the disadvantages which they faced. Billy's mother described how this tuition was just part of the overall effort which she put in to trying to maximise his potential from a very early age:

> Dr Black said that the number one thing was communication, number two was use of the hands and number three was the feet. This was the order of priority. This was a very useful piece of information. I wasn't always concentrating on, 'Will he walk?' I realised that he must do more and see more than our other children put together. Everywhere it was possible to take him, we took him. One of the earliest things I read was that the saddest thing about a disabled child was its clean hands, that they can't root around and find things that normal children do and therefore they have to have them brought to them. We had a big chair made for him and a great big tray with a rail to stop things falling off and I used to give him everything. If I found a

cabbage leaf with a snail on it or lumps of coal or pieces of dough, anything at all that I felt he'd have been able to root out for himself.

He couldn't speak at this time but I talked myself dry. I talked all the time and told him what I was doing so he'd understand everything. He looked so bright and intelligent. When he was about four I felt that I was getting bogged down. He was too young for school but I felt that if he could only learn to read; this is what he needs more than anything in life. I put an ad in the paper and asked for somebody to come and do part-time teaching. This was wonderful for him. Things just happened at the right time. But before that he'd had an operation on his leg. That was a bad experience and it set him back an awful lot. The ad was answered by a young girl and she was willing to come three afternoons a week and see what she could do with him. She came to us for a year and she did reading with him as much as she could and number work. He was always avid to learn so he lapped it up.

'Let's go down by Ailesbury Road and see the apple blossoms'

All ten in the study who had cerebral palsy had spent at least some time attending St Brendan's School, a special day school in Sandymount in Dublin which was established in 1952 by the National Association for Cerebral Palsy. However, there was quite a range of opinion among them about the service provided by this school. Some, and particularly the two who had attended ordinary primary schools, emphasised how it was vitally important to them as it represented what they considered was their only hope of receiving a formal education. Christine, for example, cringed when she thought of how backward she was academically by the time St Brendan's was established:

> So I never went back to school until the Cerebral Palsy [school] started. Oh, I was terrible, terrible, terrible. When I think back now, to think that at fourteen I was just starting off. It's really dreadful. But I was lucky. As I say, my mother used to sit down and help me a lot. It took me years to catch up as it were.

Although St Brendan's catered for pupils up to the age of eighteen years, it did not provide a structured second-level education or prepare pupils for state examinations such as the Intermediate and Leaving Certificates. This was seen as a major shortcoming among the group and they said it resulted in a rather disorientating disruption of the type of relationship between age and stage in the educational system which is strongly associated with mainstream education. Peter talked a good deal about this when recalling some of the shortcomings and highlights associated with his school days at St Brendan's in the 1950s:

> By the time I was fifteen, I ended up in what you might call sixth class. In other words, I started three more years of schooling in sixth class and there was such a variance of complaints that we couldn't have a standard. They just got you at your capability and saw how you got on from there. You know, technically we weren't children. We were seventeen, eighteen and, although we had various mentalities, we did have something in common. I forgot to tell you, we were driven to school by an entire embassy car pool – British, Canadian, American – Monday to Friday; the wives of the ambassadors were in the car pool together. One

of my favourite women was Mrs Reeves. We used to do things; this was when my real education began. She'd have a few minutes: 'Let's go down by Ailesbury Road and see the apple blossoms come out.' So we would. She made me interested in people, the way people reacted to each other. She was a very approachable person, a lovely person. We all loved her.

Five of the ten people with cerebral palsy completed their education at St Brendan's School and all these shared the view that their lack of academic qualifications was a major disadvantage in their lives. However, it must be said that they also felt that under the circumstances of their time there had been little alternative for them but to remain at this special school.

The group who moved from St Brendan's to other schools consisted of two who went to special boarding schools in England and Northern Ireland respectively and three who went as day pupils to post-primary schools in Dublin.

'It was just like the promised land'

Aisling and Billy were the two who went away to schools in England and the North of Ireland respectively. Their mothers stressed that they had been reluctant to send them away but that there were really no other options open to them. The special school which Aisling moved to did not follow a regular second level curriculum. Her mother said that she had sent her there on the advice of a medical specialist who felt that it would be good for Aisling to go away to school like her non-disabled brother and sister who were already at boarding schools in Ireland. Aisling, who suffers from cerebral palsy, said that she had liked the school in England. Her mother described it as being like 'paradise' but said that she often wondered why Aisling's academic performance had fallen far short of what had been expected on the basis of intelligence tests:

Ah, the school was out of this world. It had everything under the sun, socially everything. The headmistress was an outstanding person. Well, you'd want to be to take on that sort of thing. They had fire drill. Imagine getting them all out. They were changed for the evening meal even with the hassle of getting clothes on and off. I'm looking for her academic reports here but you can see how limited she is. She'd really need one of these, what do you call them? Eyeboards. You know her movement is so limited and she withdraws when she can't communicate. I forget what her IQ came out as. I think it came out at 120. But not if you did it now. It wouldn't come up to anything like that. As I say, I'm not Annie Sullivan, you know. Have you seen Helen Keller's life? We haven't anything like that. And I'm not superhuman and there are other children in the family but the sick one is always number one. Maybe I didn't do the right things. I don't know. I did my best.

Billy's mother said that she had sent him to school in Northern Ireland only as a last resort. She was determined that he should have the opportunity of receiving a full second level education and spoke about the many barriers which they had had to overcome in the mid-1960s before managing to achieve this:

There was no question of integrated education here in the Republic. I would look at the buildings and say, 'How would he manage in a place like that?' I felt he was so severely handicapped that somebody might feel sorry for him and take him in but that he would remain at the back of the class. I felt that the difficulties were so great that it wouldn't work. I didn't really get any help at all from his doctors about it. As he got to twelve there was no budge anywhere; nobody seemed to have any suggestions. So I wrote to a few schools in the North and in England and I had a few doctors working on the Department of Education about getting some help with funds. Then I was told that he'd have to have an IQ test done because he had to be sort of passed as being a suitable person. When the psychologist had finished doing the test, he said, 'Well obviously he has quite a high intelligence but one would question the advisability of spending a lot of money on education for him.' I nearly choked. I thought it was the most appalling, stupid, ignorant thing for a professional to say in front of him. Anyway, he really fell into the school and he was very popular with most of the teachers. The whole ambience of the place was what he had been waiting for. It was just like the promised land.

Billy himself said that he had gained a lot academically by going away to the special school in the North and was proud of the fact that he had passed his A Levels. However, he said that one of the disadvantages of going away was that he had not been able to build lasting friendships at home in Dublin during his teenage years.

'I was thrown in at the deep end'

When Brian and Jane moved from St Brendan's into second level education in Dublin in the late 1960s, they had no formal back-up and were the only people using wheelchairs in the schools they attended. Their mothers pointed out that the range of schools which was open to them was very limited because of the poor level of physical accessibility in most of the schools at that time. Both ended up going to vocational schools. For Jane, who came from an affluent background, this meant entering a social world, at sixteen years of age, which was far removed from what she was used to. Her mother talked about Jane's impact on the school and also the school's impact on her:

> Now, they were the toughest people you could imagine – boys and girls. She was hearing language that she'd never heard. They didn't stop. They treated her as one of them. It was fantastic. They didn't stop and say, 'Oh Jane, she's handicapped; Jane shouldn't be hearing this.' They just spoke as normal and pushed her around and they were absolutely marvellous. The first day she came home, she said, 'Mummy, I heard all the Fs,' and all the dreadful things. And do you know she was roaring laughing because for the first time she knew she was human. I always felt she had a great influence on that class. They all, from nothing, did extremely well.
>
> And also, if you like, not putting it snobbishly, at that time you wouldn't find anybody of – I hate to use the word 'class' – but our type in those schools and they certainly realised and they used to come up here and I used to encourage them tremendously as regards everything and they saw things maybe that they hadn't known about before. Especially the boys, they were terribly impressed and that was a revelation. I suppose they thought, here is a handicapped child trying to do *her* best and also they saw things that they wouldn't have seen if she wasn't there.

Jane herself said that she had found it very hard to make the transition from St Brendan's to the vocational school and highlighted the key role which her English teacher had played helping her to become more integrated:

I feel it cuts you off totally to be educated with only handicapped people because certainly when I went to the tech first I was thrown in at the deep end. I had never been in school with normal people. Like, for the first six months it was dreadful but after that it was super. A lot of the people are still my closest friends that went to school there. For the first six months, I'd say, I wasn't part of it but for the last year I was. There was a very open teacher there, a very nice woman actually, and she took me aside after about three or four months and said I wasn't integrating and a lot of it was my own fault. I reacted to that very badly and just said nothing. Now I'd realise but I didn't realise then that I was blaming them. So I tried to make a bit of an effort and in the English class she embarrassed me into talking more. She knew, I suppose, that I knew more than I was pretending cos I would never answer questions. Then she would ask me things straight out and it was that brought me more into things.

Brian said that he had found it difficult to keep up academically when he moved from St Brendan's to the vocational school. His mother focused on the social side of the transition and said that he had been badly bullied, and had suffered in silence, for the first two years or so, in his new school:

He did well out of the school and most of the boys in it was very good but some of them gave him a rough time. He had trouble with a few boys. I didn't know anything. It was going on for two years. They used to put plastic bags over his head and throw him down ramps in the wheelchair. He had a tough time and put up with it … Then I went to the headmaster who said it was going on for two years and people were complaining. But I hadn't been informed. He said, 'We could do nothing. You didn't come forward.' Sure I knew nothing about it and he was putting up with all that for two years. They used to threaten him that they'd run him under a bus if he said anything. At one stage they ran him down a ramp and into a wall. They done terrible things on him.

Billy and Jane both sat for Leaving Certificate exams. Jane attempted one subject only and was very pleased to pass it, especially in view of the fact that she had not been granted the extra time which she had requested for doing the exam. Billy attempted five Leaving Certificate papers and passed four. He was more than satisfied with this as it came after years of hard work and limited expectations:

> From the very beginning I was struggling to keep up the standard. I never thought I'd do the examinations. No more did my teachers or the principal of the school. But beyond all doubt, I proved to myself that my struggle was successful.

'The competition had built up already within a few days'

All those who went on to post-primary school were quite critical of the standard of education which they received at St Brendan's and of what they saw as the school's lack of emphasis on achievement and orientation towards open employment. Paul, the youngest member of this group, was most outspoken on this:

> There was no motivation from the teachers. I don't know if you know the set-up. If one wanted to go into secondary school, one had to go to England or Northern Ireland to be educated. They weren't pushy regarding education. They

thought okay when we reach eighteen we'd be shoved into the workshop area. What was the point of education? That was the general idea. See, there was no incentive to go on to secondary school. As a kid you are led by your superiors and what they say. So the teachers didn't encourage you to second level.

A pilot scheme aimed at facilitating the integration of pupils with physical disabilities into mainstream post-primary schools was introduced in two schools in Dublin and one in Cork in 1972. These schools were provided with nursing and care staff and a teacher to attend to any areas of academic or social difficulty faced by the participating pupils. This initiative was taken around the time that Paul was ready to leave St Brendan's and he moved on to one of the designated schools. He felt that the scheme worked well and that he had settled down quite quickly into the new school where he went on to take and 'scrape through' his Leaving Certificate:

> It was a big change going to the new school. There were two people with disabilities to a class and the others were ordinary students. The competition had built up already within a few days. They tried very hard to have two people with disabilities in every class so it wouldn't be felt we were alone. At first it was a strange experience. Everyone in the class was going into a new atmosphere so when I took that into account I didn't feel too bad. We were more or less all in the same boat.

'And of course everywhere you went there were barriers'

The three people with cerebral palsy who achieved most highly at post-primary level went on to attend university.

Gerry, who sustained a spinal cord injury when he was in his twenties, also experienced university as a person with a disability.

Gerry and Billy succeeded in getting degrees in college. Neither experienced much difficulty with the academic work but both said that they ran into difficulties when trying to participate in college life. Gerry stressed that there was little or no consideration given to the needs of people with disabilities at the university he attended in the 1970s:

> And, of course, everywhere you went there were barriers. I mean, a very simple example is you take the lecture theatres. You open the lecture theatre's double doors and the minute you open it there's steps down to the well of the theatre and nowhere to park a chair unless you leave the doors open and sit in the bloody hall whereupon everyone else doesn't hear the lecture and you don't hear the lecture. Another option was tape recorders. Okay, you can strap a tape recorder down on the lecturer's desk and come and collect it. They wouldn't let me do that.
>
> They also said, 'What are you going to do about exams? You can't write your exams.' They wouldn't let me tape my exams. Why not? 'Because,' they said, 'tapes can be interfered with and the externs can't cope.' All of these minor practical problems were brought forward as reasons why one couldn't participate in the process. I got a bit bolshie and dogged about it and said, 'Hump you, if this is what Joe Public can aspire to.' I've enough bloody troubles to be going on with, trying to get back into the race. And if I have the support, which I have, of a very supportive family and a great set of friends who absolutely refused to believe that life stopped there. One felt damned if one was going to be beaten by this so-called system and we actually got round it.

Billy said that his biggest problem associated with going to university related to the transport arrangements which were made for him and which virtually cut him off from the night life of the college:

> I enjoyed college but I think if I was back again I would perhaps do things differently. I think I perhaps spent too much time studying and I regret that I wasn't more involved with societies and that sort of thing. The first two years I had a taxi supplied, paid for by the Health Board. The problem with that was that the timetable was set. I was in at half eight and back at seven. If I wanted to stay on for some reason it was difficult to arrange. It was the way the Health Board organised it. I think in second year there was a bit more leeway. The taxi service was cut off in third year because of cutbacks. So my father took me in some days and then others in the area at the college gave me lifts and I paid for taxis a few times a week.

Paul and Brian were both accepted by universities in spite of not meeting the usual academic requirements for entry. Paul spent two years at college and received a certificate at the end of this time saying that he had attended lectures on a particular course. He said that his choice of subjects had been constrained because the lecture rooms used on some of the courses he was interested in were inaccessible for wheelchair users. He said that he had enjoyed his time at the university and made it clear that he had sought to avoid any confrontations over provision for people with disabilities in the college:

> If there were any difficulties I would bring them to the college authorities rather than having the Students' Union screaming about them. I think I carried on as an ordinary student avoiding any kind of protests, in general being a good boy.

57

Brian, who came from a working class background, made the decision to go to university when he was offered a scholarship by a voluntary organisation. However, he had huge problems keeping up with the academic work and left the college after about three months:

> Like in school, I was trying to pull myself up to the standard. I wasn't really at the university standard when I went to college so I knew I had so much groundwork to do and I was doing it between my studies. I possibly knew all along that no way could I piecify the joinings no matter how much I studied.

Brian's mother said that the family had been put under severe pressure in trying to pay for his keep at university. It was clear that she was pessimistic from the start about his chances of being able to complete the course:

> I didn't like it at the beginning, to tell the truth, cos I knew Brian wasn't able for it. Some man came here and he told me he was going to the college Tuesday morning. I was vexed over it because he was gone that quick. So they enlightened me that it was, I think, £500. It turned out it used to cost me £200 a month for his keep. The £500 was only for the education he got. I used to have to pay for his room and his food. He was grand in it for a while. I used to go and see him every second Sunday and then the nurse came and told me that she thought he wasn't well and could I get him taken home every weekend for a break. I got him brought home – his uncle used to go and collect him and bring him back. But then the nurse came again and told me it was all too much for him so she said, 'It's up to yourself whether you leave him or take him home.' So I took him home. He used to be up studying until one or two in the morning and then he'd be

up again at half six or seven. I found all his tablets in his luggage. He wasn't taking his tablets; he hadn't time. I was more out of pocket than what he won. It took every penny we had to keep him in it, £50 a week.

'It was a sort of con and I fell for it'

Three people in the study attended third level colleges, other than universities, after their disabling condition had been diagnosed. Eamonn, who had multiple sclerosis, was the only one of these who completed his course. He trained as a chartered accountant by being articled to a firm and attending classes at night. Although he was diagnosed as having multiple sclerosis shortly after he had embarked on his training, it was not until many years later that he actually learned that he had the disease. He stressed that he had experienced a number of problems during his training as a result of having the disease and felt that he might never have finished the course if he had known his diagnosis from the beginning:

> I qualified but it took me a few years. I used to go to classes and I'd walk from here. I used to be dragging my legs after me. I couldn't understand it. I didn't know I had MS but others knew it. I'd be walking up the road going from side to side and people on the road and neighbours would say, 'This fella Eamonn, he's at the drink again.' I didn't know at the time but I heard it afterwards. Another thing was during the exams I'd know that I wanted to go to the toilet but when I'd go to the toilet nothing might come. Sometimes I'd feel during the exam that I just had to go to the toilet. I'd put up my hand and be let out to the toilet and nothing would

happen. I'd come back and sit down again and I'd blooming want to go again and I'd say, 'Jesus, I can't get up because the invigilator will think I have a cog under the toilet and I'm going in and out to have a look at it.'

So I just went through it. I just put up with it. But, thank God, I did get the exams. I thank God I qualified as an accountant because if I was a plumber or a doctor or an electrician you would have to be very mobile. In retrospect it was probably a good thing that I wasn't told because I would have used that as an excuse. I would have been feeling very sorry for myself.

Simon also had multiple sclerosis but differed very much from Eamonn in that he knew of his suspected diagnosis from the age of seventeen. He embarked on an electronics course soon after passing his Leaving Certificate but decided to abandon it when he was about half way through it. He said that the fact of knowing that he had multiple sclerosis was the crucial factor in his decision to leave:

> After I'd been on the course for about eighteen months, I said, 'What are you doing?' I said, 'Someday this could hit you. What use is electronics going to be to you? Say you've a soldering iron in your hand and you can't grip it and it might be worth hundreds of pounds. You're just going to be thrown out.' So I gave it up. I just sort of said, 'Get out now and enjoy yourself and wait till it hits you, *if* it hits you. Always on the back of me mind, it wouldn't hit me.'

Derek, who had cerebral palsy, was still angry about his experience with an art college. He said that his artistic talent had been noticed and fostered by his teachers in St Brendan's School in Sandymount. He was most interested in water colours and painted with the brush in his mouth because he did not have the use of his hands. After leaving St Brendan's, he went for art lessons twice a week with a landscape artist who held group sessions. However, the artist moved house after about a year and Derek had to give up going to the classes because the new premises were most unsuitable for wheelchairs. Two years later, his hopes were raised by an art college which claimed to be interested in training people with disabilities. However, Derek felt that this was mere tokenism and left the college after about a year and a half with a great sense of disillusionment:

> I found an article about this college and the boss said, 'We'd take any disabled people that would come to us.' So I said, 'Right, here's one comin'.' Anyway, I made an appointment and he couldn't fault me at me paintings but they didn't want me so they had to find a way of getting rid of me without causing trouble. So there were a few there as well as him. And they were there, 'How would you get up the stairs?' Well the staircase could bring three wheelchairs up it side by side they are so wide. So he said, 'There's an awful lot of trouble. The teachers don't want the trouble of asking pupils to help you out.'
>
> So I went away, I went off. Then I was tellin' a friend about it and I said, 'What the hell, so I footed it back to the college and said to the boss, 'Didn't you say that you'd take people with disabilities?' So this time he said, 'All right.' He fooled me though. There was a catch which I didn't see. See, they let me in but I ended up in a class of people that had qualified in their own fields, not art, and they were just doing extra. Among the seventeen of them, there wasn't one that had ever done painting. There was nobody to help me or show me how to do painting. There were people to hold paints for me. That's why I was put in there. It was a sort of con and I fell for it.
>
> I really fell for it. So then they got a brilliant idea. They

would build a chair for me so that everything would be automatic. I wouldn't have to have anybody beside me for painting. They spent about £400 just to get the basic shape of the chair. They said, 'There's no point in you coming back until we've finished the chair.' So I left and I heard nothing, absolutely nothin' and I bumped into a fella in town who was on the design team. He said, 'When you left it was forgotten, that was it.' So that was the end of that. Forget it, son.

'If I'd got a Leaving Cert. that would have stood to me even now'

The range of educational qualifications among the thirty people involved in the study was quite broad. Four held either degrees or diplomas at third level; another nine had passed exams at second level; and seventeen had left school with no qualifications at all.

The people with spinal cord injury had marginally more educational qualifications than those with either cerebral palsy or multiple sclerosis. However, when comparing the three groups, the most striking point is that those with cerebral palsy had far more involvement with the educational system than those with spinal cord injury or multiple sclerosis. All ten people with cerebral palsy remained in some form of education until they were at least eighteen years old. In contrast, seven of those with multiple sclerosis and five with spinal cord injury had dropped out of the educational system by the age of fifteen.

All seven with multiple sclerosis who left school early were women and they all said that they had had to leave because of their family's financial circumstances. Helen was fairly typical of these:

I never knew my father. He had died when I was a year old. I was the youngest of what was a large family but had dwindled down to five by the time I had come along. They died as two or three year olds from meningitis. I'd say two of them died from meningitis and my father, he died from TB. Then my eldest sister, the oldest of the lot, she died from TB. This was in the years when TB was as MS is today; there wasn't a thing for it. Schooling was just an ordinary little school which I went to and left when I was thirteen and a half so that I could bring in more money.

Three of the four people with spinal cord injury who left school at an early age were men and all these said that they had disliked school intensely and had wanted to leave as early as possible. Al was among these and recalled his school days in the following way:

School was non-existent for me really cos I was a total dunce; me and a mate – two dunces. We were only able to just about cope and we were kinda neglected. We had a bad teacher. I put it down to the system then. As far as school was concerned, I can't ever remember doing a homework properly; any that I did were wrong. The help at home was non-existent. As a matter of fact, we used to copy our homework from the guys who had it right. I really hated school so much that all I wanted was to get out and work. Nothing like having money in your pocket.

Eddie was really the only person who seemed to feel that he might have made a mistake leaving school relatively early. He had left after passing the Group Certificate because he wanted to pursue a particular trade. He had already qualified in this when his accident occurred and had been forced out of it because of his disability. He subsequently got a job at a low level in the civil service hierarchy and felt that his lack of educational qualifications had come back to haunt him:

> I'm going to study this year to get up as far as a clerical officer, then hopefully an executive officer later on. But I'll have to go back to school and do the Leaving and everything. If I had been a bit cuter now earlier on - like before the accident - I should have done night classes really and if I'd got a Leaving Cert. that would have stood to me even now.

Summary

This chapter has focused on the educational histories of the people in the study. It has been particularly concerned with finding out about the experiences of the thirteen people who were involved in the educational system as pupils or students with disabilities. What sorts of opportunities were open to them? What difficulties did they encounter?

These questions were answered by each individual concerned, with reference to the point in history at which he or she was involved with the educational system. The educational careers of this group as a whole spanned the mid-1940s to the mid-1970s. This was a period which saw much progress in educational provision for people with significant physical disabilities. Those who entered the educational system in the mid-1940s pointed out that there were no satisfactory options open to them. They could either go to residential hospital schools or to ordinary schools in which there were no special provisions made for them. These older respondents saw the development of special day schools in the mid-1950s as a major step forward.

All ten people with cerebral palsy had some experience of at least one of these special day schools – St Brendan's in Sandymount, Dublin. The younger respondents, in particular, were critical of the special school system in Ireland because they saw it as both shaping and reflecting the very limited expectations which they perceived as being widely held about the academic potential of people with significant physical disabilities.

Those who went on to attend second level schools felt that they had achieved this in spite, rather than because, of prevailing attitudes within the educational system. The four who succeeded in passing state examinations considered that they had surpassed most people's expectations of them.

On the whole, those with cerebral palsy were much less concerned about the issue of segregated as opposed to integrated education than they were about having the opportunity of being prepared for state examinations at second level. They all saw educational qualifications as being of vital importance in relation to securing employment and felt that people with significant disabilities were doubly disadvantaged in the labour market if they did not have a high standard of education behind them.

It was striking that those with cerebral palsy had far more involvement with the educational system than those with either multiple sclerosis or spinal cord injury. All ten had remained in either school or college until they were at least eighteen years old. On the other hand, seven of those with multiple sclerosis and five with spinal cord injury had dropped out of school and taken up employment by the age of fifteen. It must be remembered that most of these people had already left school before the free post-primary education scheme was introduced in Ireland in 1967.

CHAPTER 4

TRAINING AND EMPLOYMENT

It would be difficult to overestimate the importance which is attached to employment in Irish society today. The term 'employment' relates to far more than how people occupy their time and earn their living; it harks back to the very core of personal identity and the question of how we measure an individual's social worth.

This chapter seeks to answer a number of key questions regarding the views and experiences of people with physical disabilities in relation to the world of work. These questions concern: the importance of *paid* employment; the impact of the onset of disability on a person's employment history; the relationship between educational/training background and employment prospects; the role of sheltered training and employment; the experience of unemployment; how disability affects domestic labour; and finally, people's contact with vocational assessment and placement agencies.

'If you measure it in a material sense, I'm a nothing, you know'

The Irish social welfare system was built on the idea that people with significant physical disabilities should be exempt from work. Traditionally, they were seen as part of the dependant population which had to be supported by the 'fit' members of society. So, how did the people with physical disabilities in this study perceive their role in relation to the economy? It is impossible to generalise when answering this question because a whole range of perspectives manifested themselves.

Nine of the thirty participants in the study were in some form of paid employment at the time of interview and a further six defined themselves as being unemployed and strongly oriented towards securing 'proper' employment. Everyone in this group stressed that paid employment was very important to them and Eoin, who had become unemployed after his accident, was particularly emphatic on this:

> At the moment I'm determined to get a job and I can't get one. I think I'd work better than someone else because I'd be more dedicated and more willing and more happy to have a job. I know people out there that won't work – they won't take a job. I'd take it.

Four of those who were in employment were self-employed. All these saw self-employment as less desirable than being employed by someone else but felt that it was really the only option open to them. Brian, for example, who had cerebral palsy, spoke of how he had reluctantly moved into a small self-employment venture after years of trying to find open employment:

The attitude on the whole towards disabled people is pretty negative. People aren't willing to study the real circumstances of your disability. I think that employers and personnel people look on me as mentally handicapped. When they look at me and I ask them to employ me I'd rather they'd ask me, 'What can you do, what do you suffer from?' so as I can give them the true picture of myself rather than leave them form their own. I was looking for a job everywhere and anywhere. I even tried London, New Zealand, America, everywhere. I finally realised that it's the employers' market and they are out to grab people who they see as being effectively able to do the work. I just realised, well, I will go my own way.

Hugh was the only person in paid employment who had not experienced problems in relation to finding work. This was because his employers decided to keep his job open for him after his accident. He felt that he had been very fortunate in this:

I was working before I had the accident and the job was kept open for me. I lost the rank of manager because of me accident. They held the job open for me and that was a great thing. I was in hospital when I heard. The managers and the directors and all were up to see me. One of them said, 'Look, don't worry about the job, it's there.' I never got a chance to worry about it and think about it cos when I was in hospital the job was the last thing I thought of. It was me I was thinking of, the family or whatever. I wasn't thinking about work and they kinda said it to me before I got a chance to think about it. That was one thing in me favour. It was great not to have to go out and look for employment when I came out of hospital.

All four people who had managed to find employment as people with disabilities said that they had had to work hard to secure it and that they had gone through many crises of confidence before they had eventually found employers who were willing to take them on. Jane was the only person with cerebral palsy who was in full-time paid employment. Ironically, she attributed her success in getting her post as a receptionist largely to the fact that she had felt she had no hope of winning the job competition for it:

After I did the Leaving, I did nothing for a year. God, I was looking for a job from day one but there was nothing. Then, a friend of my father's gave me a part-time job which I didn't really like very much because, I mean, I knew he was only giving me the job because he was a friend of my father. So I got on to the Rehabilitation Board and they sent me for five interviews in six months. You see, when I went to the interview for this job, I thought I hadn't a hope of getting it cos there was another girl there wheeling herself around so I said, 'This is it. She has the job.' To me, you know, she was spinning herself around and they would have to have someone to wheel me around but I think that was why I got it because I was so confident when I went in. I was cheeky nearly cos I was sure I wasn't going to get the job cos it was very stiff. The job is great. I love it because I feel it's a job that someone else would have to do if I wasn't there. In other words, it's a real job. It's a busy switch-board so I love it. I'm there six years and I've hardly missed a day.

The other fourteen people in the study who were strongly oriented towards paid employment shared Jane's aspiration towards wanting to contribute to society rather than being dependent on it. Peter, who had cerebral palsy and who was unemployed after giving up on a small self-employment venture, was most articulate on this as he reflected on his career:

Fifteen years I actually did work, you know. I got browned off with the whole thing. No way it ever made any money. Technically, I've had a good if unproductive life. If you measure it in a material sense, I'm a nothing, you know. There's too many people making it easy for me to be an entertaining clown. I'm the big one at the party. I hear it all the time, 'Jasus, listen to him, you'd swear he'd gone to college.' Sure half the bloody idiots I've seen come out of college don't know half of what I know. But how do you use it? That's my problem. People are going around saying that they don't want to use human beings and I'm saying, 'Use me, use me.' I can't, I haven't a hook. I can't hook into anything.

Fifteen of the thirty people in the study were not oriented towards paid employment at the time of interview and their reasons for this were quite varied. Seven were women with multiple sclerosis who had withdrawn from the labour force to work in the home before becoming affected by the disease. Four of these had left their employment when they got married. The other three had continued working until the birth of their second child and Helen's experience was quite typical of these:

I worked in factories from when I was about fourteen. Then I went into various shops. I left work for a while after I got married but then I went back and stuck it out until my first baby was born. I didn't go back to work after that for about two years. Then my husband went away to work. We were living with his mother, by the way. She encouraged me to go back to work. She said she would mind the children and of course I took the opportunity and went back. Then my husband came home; he was nine months away. When he came back I left work again because I became pregnant straightaway and then I had my second little boy and I gave up work after that baby was born.

Two of those with spinal cord injuries had received substantial compensation awards and said that they were not interested in pursuing the possibility of finding paid employment. Both were very significantly disabled and emphatic that some form of occupation was essential to give them a purpose in life. Danny was doing a course run for people with disabilities at the time of interview and Conor was attending and enjoying a day centre which he went to on three days each week:

> For eight months after I came out of hospital I was at home just going out visiting here and there. I used to go down the road in the chair and for some reason or another I noticed vans coming round the corner with chairs and I saw them a few times in different weeks. I said, 'Whatever it is, it's something round that corner.' So I detoured round and I saw it. I went into the office and the girl said, 'Did you hear about this place?' 'Actually I didn't, I said. 'This is a day centre here,' she said. 'We'll take you in for assessment.' I was delighted with meself. All of a sudden I had a place to go. It's a great place.

Christine, Aisling, Dave and Larry were others who were involved in sheltered work situations and not in any way oriented towards open employment. The first three had cerebral palsy and had gone straight from special school into sheltered employment. Larry, in contrast, had multiple sclerosis and had only recently begun attending a day centre after being forced to give up various jobs due to his deteriorating condition.

Finally, Paula and Simon also belonged to the group who were not oriented towards paid employment. Paula, who was one of the oldest people with cerebral palsy, was living in a nursing home. She had had some experience of sheltered work after leaving special school and was most anxious to make the point that people with physical disabilities, however significant their disabilities may be, do not want to be exempted or excluded from making a contribution to society:

> We don't want to be forgotten about just because we're disabled. You want to feel that you are doing something. Even if you never did anything, you want to feel that you are of some use.

Simon was also in residential care; he had multiple sclerosis and felt that his working days were over because of his condition. However, he drew some satisfaction from the knowledge that he had worked for as long as possible and in places which he loved:

> Jobs were plentiful at the time. You know, I'd work for maybe six months – I never collected the dole – get the money together, go on holiday, come back and take a job. It was only once in me life that I really got broke. A friend and I went into a pub and we were a penny short for a bottle of lemonade and we just looked at each other and said, 'That's it.' We both got jobs, got enough money together and hit Paris. Waitered in cafés in Paris and from that we went around Europe. We just kept moving. I went to London. That's the best city in the world. It's a place I'd love to be now. I really enjoyed being over there.

'I just want to make a go of it'

Few people expect to be struck down by a disabling condition when they are in their late teens, twenties or thirties. Instead, they generally see these as years in which they will launch their careers and establish themselves in the adult world. What then of those who do meet disability? What impact does it have on their employment situations?

The experiences of the ten people with spinal cord injury in this study and two of the men with multiple sclerosis are particularly relevant when seeking answers to these questions. Although the various people in this group had acquired their disabilities at relatively young ages, they had accumulated between them many years of employment experience while still able-bodied. This was largely due to the fact that most of them had left school early and started working immediately. Seven of the twelve had worked in countries other than Ireland and all these depicted their time abroad as having been exciting and full of adventure. For example, Eoin, who was injured in an accident in his early twenties, said:

> I was sort of a wildish sort of head when I was younger. We were mad at that time – around fifteen or sixteen. I went to London when I was sixteen for two years. I did a lot of things other people wouldn't do. I went with three or four other people and we had a great time. I got a job over there. I was sixteen and you had to be twenty to get it. I didn't look anything like twenty when I was sixteen and I had to go past the medical test and all to get it.

All ten people with spinal cord injuries were working as paid employees for various companies and businesses when their accidents occurred. The dividing line between being disabled and not being disabled is harder to identify in the case of those with multiple sclerosis because of the nature of the disease. What can be said with certainty is that Eamonn and Larry were in employment before they knew they had MS or were significantly affected by it.

The onset of disability caused a major disruption in the working lives of these twelve people. At the time of interview only six of them were still in some form of paid employment while the others were either unemployed, or in sheltered employment of some description. Of those who were in employment, Hugh was the only one who was still working for his previous employer. As we saw in the last section, he felt fortunate to have been kept on in his job in spite of losing his managerial status. He stressed that he had found it difficult going back to work after his accident and that he had been very sensitive and embarrassed particularly about his bladder problems:

> I went back to work about six or eight weeks after I got out of hospital. I was out for a long time and I decided I'd like to get back – start off again. It was completely different, mind you, in the chair. I felt completely different. It's the same really now because everyone up there has got used to me being in the chair. I don't feel any different now. An awful lot of people don't realise the problems you have in a wheelchair. I have bladder problems; bladder control, I simply don't have it. I wear a bag thing. And if I had a problem with that it used to bother me, mainly because people didn't realise that you'd have it. They didn't know what it was. Now, the people in the job, they know.
>
> I was lucky actually; the general manager's wife's sister is in a wheelchair and he understood. I was lucky in that sense that I had at least one of the managers I could talk to about problems I had or might have. I, in fact, went to him one day and talked about problems that I might have; problems I knew I possibly could have because I was in the chair and because of the lack of bladder control; problems that might

arise – some of them did, some of them didn't – but I put it all down on the line to him. I said, 'This, this and this could happen,' and he said, 'I know.' It made it that bit easier.

Eddie was the only one of those who had changed their places of employment after the onset of disability who said that he had hoped to return to work for his previous employer in at least some capacity. He had actively pursued the possibility of being retained by his employer and felt particularly disappointed when this had not come to pass:

> I had been in the job for three years and the manager knew me pretty well. He was saying, 'We could retrain you into the office end of things, salaries and that.' Then I had to ring the head boss man about something and I said that the manager had arranged for me to try and get back to work in the office in the same place. He turned round and said, 'What makes you think that Mr Hickey can give you a job back? That's up to me.' 'Oh Jesus,' I said, 'now, I'm after putting me foot in it.'
>
> Of course, Mr Hickey was away on holidays. When he came back he got on to me and said, 'The cheek of you ringing the boss like that when I'm away on holidays, behind me back and mentioning the job.' I had understood all the time that it was all in negotiation. I had been in with Hickey a few times. Even up to the week before he went on holidays, he was bringing me to lunch and everything. I thought everything was going smooth until this. The worst mistake was ringing the boss. That squashed everything. So it turned out I don't get me job back and there was abuse hurled at me on the 'phone from Hickey.

Those who had not tried to continue working for their previous employers gave a variety of reasons for this. Al said that the geographical location of his pre-injury work did not suit him. Gerry and Paddy said that they had no interest in the type of work which would have been on offer given their injuries. Eamonn, who had multiple sclerosis, said that he had reached a point where it was impossible for him to continue working outside his own home. As his condition had deteriorated he had moved from work involving a good deal of travel to tutoring students in mathematics from home:

> As you know about accountancy, you have to go from place to place doing audits. I used to have to pre-plan everything. For example, I'd know that this disability I had with the waterworks could come at any stage so some of the kind of places you would go there mightn't be a toilet there at all. So where do you go? So I had to plan. Like, if it was O'Connell Street, okay, the Gresham Hotel was there so I'd go to the Gresham or things like that. It was always pre-planned. I used to drive the car for work and the funny thing driving the car was when I was moving I was fine but to stop at lights I'd get dizzy. I used to have to try and plan it so that I'd keep moving all the time. It could mean going ten miles to go fifty yards. It was gas.
>
> Now that I'm working from home things still have to be planned. But the plans can go awry because of the physical thing. For example, I might have a student coming in this afternoon and I'd say, 'Listen, would you ever ring me this morning because I don't know if I'll be able to see or not, how the vision will be. I probably will, but just to confirm.'

Gerry and Al had also made the shift from being employees before their accidents to being self-employed afterwards. Gerry was a freelance consultant and said that he needed the flexibility which self-employment allowed because of problems with pressure sores:

I couldn't predict that I would be a nine to five user of a job. Flexibility is what I need in relation to the chair. Whereas now I'm more or less back on par, four or five years ago I wasn't. It's only in the last two years that I can allow sitting sixteen or seventeen hours a day in the chair.

Al had worked in the construction field before his accident and had decided that the best way to accommodate his disability was to set up a small manufacturing business in which he would be able to use his existing skills in metalwork. He was in severe financial difficulty at the time of interview and was unable to afford to take on assistance which he felt he really needed. However, he was still determined to succeed:

I want to be as independent as possible, forget about the wheelchair. I just want to make a go of it. I think it would be a great inspiration to other people as well to see that a guy in a wheelchair can set up a workshop. I have a bit of a problem with big sheets of eight-by-four but I can get the boys in the workshop next door to help me with them. If there's no one around and I have to put a big sheet on the table, I'll find some way – fingernails and teeth – it goes up there.

The onset of disability did not just result in changes in employment status and place of employment. It also brought changes for some in the type of work which they were involved in. Eamonn, Hugh and Al remained working in similar fields to those of their pre-disability days. However, Eddie, Paddy and Gerry had moved into totally new fields after their accidents. For each of them, this meant starting at the bottom of the ladder and learning new skills. Eddie, who changed from skilled manual work to an administrative job in the civil service, stressed that it was frustrating to have to begin the process of career-building all over again:

Other people say, 'Ah you're in the Civil Service; you're on great pay.' Five years ago I was coming out with double what I get now. You have to have the Leaving Cert. to get an Executive Officer's job. I've been out of school since 1972 so how in God's name do I get back up to the level of a fellow with honours in the Leaving? Even to look at the maths me young sisters are doing I wouldn't have a clue where to start. To be honest with you, I'll have to go back and start from scratch and really try and claw me way back up to the standard nowadays.

'What use is some bugger who can quote Shakespeare, anyway?

A strong educational background is considered by many to be the key to securing employment in Ireland. How then does educational background seem to affect the employment prospects of people with physical disabilities?

The experience of the people in the study suggests that a person's past education and training are indeed very significant in relation to employment. For example, it emerged that all eight people who were in paid employment at the time of interview had passed state examinations at either second or third level. Three of these, Eddie, Al and Paddy, had also completed apprenticeships in particular trades before the onset of their disabilities.

Having a good educational background was by no means a guarantee of employment. Rather, it seemed that where a person had a second or third level education, more employment options were available and career changes were much easier to make. Also, it appeared that level of education was more important than severity of disability when it came to employment. Billy and Gerry, for example, who had university degrees, were in employment at the time of interview in spite of being amongst the most disabled in the study as a whole.

On the other hand, people like Peter, Kevin and Christine, who were much less disabled, had had little or no success in the employment field. They attributed this very largely to their lack of educational qualifications in a society which places considerable emphasis on qualifications, as well as to the negative attitudes which exist towards people with disabilities. This was how Peter, who had cerebral palsy and who had completed his schooling at St Brendan's special school some twenty-five years earlier, accounted for his difficulties in relation to finding employment:

> The environment, the attitudes of people had a lot to do with it. I did the basic three Rs and the rest of my education consisted of bumming around the street mixing with bad lots and getting into trouble. In that way if anyone asks me am I educated, I say, 'Yes I am, bloody well educated. I have no bits of paper to prove that I can quote Shakespeare. What use is some bugger who can quote Shakespeare, anyway? Now if I try putting myself on the job market as a typist/telephonist, there's also about five thousand kids just leaving school who will get there first, not because they are any better at the typewriter than me but because they have bits of paper saying they left school. And employers seem to have gotten rid of the notion, 'Ah, give him a month's trial; if you work out, you work out'. I wish they'd bring it back because it's the only way I'd get a job. If I could get someone to say, 'Look, I'll give you a month's trial, no promises,' I'm sure I could get a job. But the kids come out with degrees; they are lousy typists anyway but once they're employed they can't really be fired.

None of the five who completed their education at special schools which did not prepare pupils for second level examinations went on to enter open employment. In fact, Peter was the only one of these who had been strongly oriented towards paid employment and vehemently against sheltered work. The others had all gone more or less straight from special school into some form of sheltered employment. Christine recalled how she had finally moved away from special school after she had been refused payment for 'work' which she had been doing there:

> We were only allowed to stay in school till we were eighteen. I never did my Leaving or anything like that. I still got physio there everyday until I was twenty-one. That was the only reason I was still going and then we used to get our dinner every day and I used to help out with the babies or with any of them that couldn't feed themselves. I'd help to feed them at lunch time and things like that; or help with washing dishes or whatever. I did ask them could they pay me a little something in the week to help me have some pocket money of my own. I felt I wanted something of my own but I wanted to work for it. Okay, I felt I was entitled to something when one of the girls was already getting paid for just peeling the potatoes but I was helping them in the toilet or feeding them or whatever and I felt why shouldn't I get something as well but I was turned down. So I got fed up and went off for myself and got in touch with the Rehabilitation and they took me on.

While educational qualifications certainly seemed to be of enormous benefit to those seeking open employment, there was a downside to this education/employment equation. This took the form of major frustration in those who, in spite of having solid educational qualifications, could not secure open employment. Brian and Paul, who had cerebral palsy, were the epitome of this. Both had attended second-level schools in the hope of securing open employment. However, neither had achieved this after many years of trying and were bitterly disappointed. Brian's mother said that she had never expected him to get work and had tried to prevent him from raising his hopes too much about his employment prospects:

> The doctor told me that he'd never work and I knew. I used to try and explain to him but I could never get it to sink in, never. He was too determined; very determined he is. But he couldn't get work. Now he done two Leavings and it was hard to look at him. You'd feel sorry for him sitting here with nothing to do and he did try very, very hard. All he wanted was a wage package. That's all he wanted was a package; to say that he was after earning that.
>
> I never minded him not working because I knew he wasn't going to work myself but he thought he should have went out like the others. It never bothered me. Now he used to do a course and he used to go out of here at eight o'clock in the morning and it would be lashing rain and now I would have preferred him to stop in bed. I felt sorry for him going out in that weather, like on a cold bitter rainy morning. That's the way I was about him. I used to feel sorry for him going out. I often said it, 'I don't think you should go out on a morning like this.' 'I'm going out to work. I'm no different, you know.' To me, he's just the same as the others. I don't always think of him as handicapped.

'I said I'd go and give it a bash'

The period since the late 1940s has seen the development of a wide range of sheltered training and employment centres for people with disabilities in Ireland. These cover the whole spectrum of activity from highly structured skills training programmes to occupational therapy in day care centres. Sixteen of the thirty people in the study had at least some experience of this 'special' provision and they had a good deal to say about it.

Eddie and Al were the only people who had been involved in full-time skills training for people with disabilities. Al completed his one-year programme but Eddie left his two-year course on office procedures at the half-way stage to take up a job in the Civil Service. He said that he had found the course interesting and that he had got on very well with the other trainees:

> There was about ten of us doing the course and most were in wheelchairs. We had good crack but I always knew from early on I'd be leaving before it was over cos I'd applied for the Civil Service job. We had got to the exam stage when I was called up; so anyway I got honours in book-keeping and accountancy so I got me script. The course was part of some body in education and they had set the standard. When I got word from the Civil Service, ah, I was over the moon. The course was definitely useful and it gave me something to do for that year. Otherwise I'd probably have gone off me rocker here at home.

Five of the others had done short training courses run for people with disabilities which lasted for about two or three months. Eoin was involved in one of these at the time of interview and was not very happy with it for various reasons:

It's a lecture course – just something to prepare you on how to get a job. I think it's twelve weeks. It's to prepare you to try and get a job after that. That's no use to me. I even told them. I said, 'That's not worth a shit.' I said, 'If there's no manual work …'. I thought it would be something with computers. I said, 'It's not computers or manual work, is it?' He said, 'No.' I said, 'I think it's a waste of bleedin' time – coming down here and getting lectures off you.' I said, 'Am I gettin' paid for it?' He said, 'No.' I said, 'What is it? I've to go down there and work for nothin', sit there and listen to all you lecturing, for nothin?' He says, 'Yeh.'

I've been out now for a few days sick and I'm in two minds about going back because I'm not getting any benefit out of it. I mean, if I knew there was a job down the road or that they'd take a person in a wheelchair, it'd be different. There's about fifteen doing the course altogether and ninety per cent of those is spastic. There's even one or two people walking around with a limp. I think I'm the only one in a wheelchair from a motor crash and I feel a little bit funny. Even if they offered you £50 a week or even £30, you'd be gettin' something. When it comes to Friday down in this place where I'm doing the course now, they're all getting their bleedin' pay cheques and what am I getting – a lift bleedin' home with nought in me pocket.

Three of those with cerebral palsy had been in sheltered work situations since leaving St Brendan's special school. Each of these seemed quite oblivious to the sheltered/open employment distinction which preoccupied people like Eoin and Paul and said that they enjoyed the challenges and fun associated with their work. Christine, who had most experience of sheltered employment, remembered the hard work and camaraderie of her first placement in the late 1950s:

They used to make things for the Health Board and things for shops in town. They did lining for skirts and coats and suits and you'd have to finish them off. I often had to hand sew the lining and all that type of thing. And the dressing gowns, you would be making summer dresses in the winter and dressing gowns in the summer. I don't know if you've ever seen them. You know the real black, heavy, hairy stuff for men's dressing gowns – the weight of it. It would weigh a ton and we used to be sweating in the summer time doing them.

They used to do nurses' hats and nuns' bathing suits. I don't know what nuns do now but then the bathing-suits were plain navy and had these enormous skirts and had all these pleats and underneath was this pants that came down to there and the leg of them was about that width. And the front came up around to the neck. Sure, if you got into the water in them – actually I have a photo somewhere of Kathleen in one of them. She got in to it one day. She did it for a laugh and we took photographs. If you got into the water in it you'd sink to the bottom, honestly. It was dreadful. You know like you'd see in the films.

In contrast to people like Christine, Simon, who had multiple sclerosis, was very disenchanted by his fleeting experience of sheltered work:

The girl I was going with eventually got through to me to get a job. So eventually after two years I decided to try and get a job. I went to the NRB and he said, 'We'll try this place and that place,' and eventually I was told about a workshop. I said I'd go and give it a bash. I went to the workshop anyway and I think I lasted half a day. I went to the girl and I said, 'What do you think you're dealing with, zombies?' Do you know what it was? It was near Easter – putting the boxes together for Easter eggs. I said I wanted to see someone and I read the manager guy. He said, 'We're providing a service.'

I said, 'Of all the Easter egg boxes that are being put together out there, are you giving the people back the money that you are getting out of it?' He said, 'No, we have to keep some of it to maintain the service; we are giving a service. We are getting people out of their homes – at least we don't have them idle in their houses all day.' I mean, it was mindless; you were putting boxes together. I couldn't believe it.

I really pity disabled people if that's the kind of thing they have to put up with. I mean, they are paying them in the region of £5 or £6 a week for that kind of stuff. There are various other places that do similar stuff – collating bits of paper and different thrash like that. It's not taking your mind off anything; it's just mindless work.

Six of the people in the study were attending day centres for at least one half day each week and most enjoyed this experience. Anne was among these and said that she had been reluctant to go at the beginning but was now happy that she had:

In the beginning, I can tell you, I was forced into it but for me own good in the end, I know that. I felt embarrassed with the ambulance pulling up out there and getting wheeled out and being up on the hoist – Cape Canaveral – but now I look forward to going. I go up there every Monday morning around ten o'clock and I'm there until about three. We make a few purses. They have a clamp for me and they clamp it on to the table up there. The room we have is lovely. The fellow that designed it had wheelchairs in mind. We make purses, key rings; another man up there, he paints ornaments for the garden. There's usually six of us. Dina is the only one that we can see coming on since we joined. When we went up first she used just sit, you wouldn't get a word out of her mouth. Now you can't hold her down. We're all ould ones and ould fellas. There was a young lad but I think he's finished because he was too young for us. John says he's the sickest of any of us, he could have a heart attack like that and we say, 'Jesus, you'd better not have it over here with us on a Monday.'

Deirdre, who was in her fifties and had MS, was much less enthusiastic about the day centre which she was attending:

All my days are the very same except Tuesday now that I go to the Centre but I'm not really keen on that cos you're sitting around and they're playing bingo and that. The car comes for me at about a quarter to twelve and I get me dinner down there for twenty pence, which nearly always I can't eat because it's bacon and stuff like that. They had me in hospital on a low cholesterol diet and the sweet does be ice cream which I can't eat either and fruit salad. Well I can eat the fruit. I do be glad when I see him coming to go home to tell the truth.

I think I'm the youngest there more or less. You should see the people able to get up and do dancing an' all. They are able to waltz and that. There's one woman there and she's able to do a jig and do a hornpipe and all and she's in her eighties. They are all very nice people but they are all old. I suppose it's meself. They do say, which I hate, 'Ah, God help her and she's so young.' I have heard them say that and even the other day they were saying that. Pity and me never did see eye to eye.

Larry, who had multiple sclerosis, was attending a day centre at the time of interview and said that he enjoyed going there once a week for 'the chat' with other people who were in a similar situation to himself. He had tried going to a sheltered workshop before the day centre but had left because he objected to being mixed in with people who were 'disturbed and mentally handicapped'.

Eoin, who was in his late twenties and disabled due to a spinal cord injury, had also had experience of feeling misplaced but in his case this occurred in a day centre catering mainly for elderly people:

> The NRB got me to go to a place at the other side of town. I went over for a day and there was about six ould ones and six ould fellas, bleedin' senile and the food droppin' out of their mouths and me there on me tod. I was just hangin' around with these ould fellas and ould ones just to get out for the day. They're wantin' to get you out for the day; send you to this bleedin' hole and sit down there with a whole load of ould fellas and ould ones eatin' their dinner and dribblin'. I don't like sayin' it but that's the way it was.

'No one wants to give me a job in a wheelchair'

Six of the people in the study considered themselves to be 'unemployed' or 'able and willing to work' at the time of interview. All these were strongly oriented towards open employment and were quite opposed to going into any form of sheltered work. Paul's mother, for example, described his ongoing objection to sheltered employment:

> Let's face it, the normal people can't get jobs and even before the recession we didn't ever expect that he would go to a job like and he certainly didn't want a workshop or a day centre. They were out because he said they were only taking you out of your own house for a few hours, I suppose to give the parents a break, and you did nothing for the day. And you see when he would be assessed, 'What can he do?' This is what

they say to you, 'What can he do?' you know. And nothing just came of anything. So anything that has been done for him has been done through ourselves – trying to get him fixed up. Jobwise, I don't know. Well, I don't know, maybe eventually. Maybe the computer or that.

There was a strong sense among those who were unemployed that they could easily get places in sheltered situations. However, it was 'real' work which they wanted. Peter, who had cerebral palsy, was quite emphatic about this:

A long time ago someone started the Rehabilitation Institute which dragged a few cripples off to dig cabbages and learn horticulture and all the rest of it. Give the man his due; he was rough and ready. Then, of course, the NRB was set up with government backing. Now what the NRB has done is to create a huge office structure, a huge image builder. None of them have been able to find me a job. All I want is a job. I don't want to know about training programmes. Training programmes just keep social workers in business.

Five of the six who were unemployed had no educational qualifications and they all felt that this compounded their difficulties in getting work. Kevin, who had sustained a spinal cord injury in the early 1960s, was quite adamant that there was little hope for people with disabilities unless they had a good education and training:

I worked for a while after me accident but it wasn't worth working because you lost your disability allowance. People in wheelchairs get pittance like even though you're doing the same job as everyone else. In one job I was doing the very same job as the person beside me. He was able-bodied. There was no difference in the work. I was doing the same as him and he was getting three times my wages. I had applied for a grant for a car. That's why I stuck it so long. You had to have six months working before you got a grant. So then I chucked it in. That was the end of that. I didn't work since. I certainly don't see meself getting a job at this stage. No way would you get a job. You would if you were specialised – computers or something like that. People going on eighteen and nineteen; they won't employ someone in a wheelchair if they can get someone like that. You'd want to be specialised.

Both Peter and Derek, who had cerebral palsy, had been self-employed before becoming unemployed. Peter had given up his business because it had run into financial difficulty. Derek, on the other hand, had been doing well as a street fund-raiser working on a commission basis. He had been forced to give up this activity because he was regularly being robbed of his daily takings. Like Peter, he felt that his working days were over because it was most unlikely that any other employment opportunities would open up for him:

I was selling tickets in town for a few years. You'd work from around nine o'clock in the morning to seven in the evening. It paid me to do it because people wouldn't buy from any one else but me. I've been told that. Then the robbing got really bad. There wasn't a thing I could do about it cos if you did say anything they'd throw you out of the chair. It's very hard to believe but this can happen at eleven o'clock in the morning in down-town Dublin and nobody would help you. People just walked on. The only people that helped me were the cops but they were never there just when you needed them. When business was really bad you might get £25 a day. It sounds good but not for the amount of work you'd do. Then I used to be robbed about twice a week and if I was robbed I had to put my own money in to make up their money. It wasn't worth it. See, unless I know a mad employer I'll never get a job and the only other way I'd get a job would be to start me own business and to do that you have to have lolly.

Dolores, who was disabled since sustaining a spinal cord injury when she was seventeen, was the only woman who defined herself as being unemployed. She was anxious to return to work now that her children were reared but felt that negative attitudes regarding her disability, age and lack of qualifications would militate against her:

> I tried to go about a job. The NRB man came to see me a good few times. He sent me papers to do an exam for a key-punch operator but there were three hundred and fifty going for it and only five jobs. I would have loved to get it. It would have been terrific; the money was good and everything. You'd get three months training an' all. Really, there isn't much hope. I mean ordinary people can't get jobs and me age is against me now. I think the worst thing people in wheelchairs suffer from is being closed in; closed in by society, I mean. There's a lot of people in wheelchairs does work in workshops and the wages they get is appalling. Now they are trained to do a job but when it comes to getting them employed in society, they won't take them because they're in a wheelchair. Isn't that wrong? It's very closed in like. They won't give them a chance.

Eoin, who was injured in a car crash, was the only unemployed person who had attended second level school. He had passed the Group Certificate before leaving school to work in a variety of jobs in both Ireland and England. He was very angry about his inability to secure work and, like all the other unemployed people, laid a lot of blame on what he considered were the harshly discriminatory attitudes of employers in this country:

I'm well able to work if someone would give me a job. I can read, I can write, no sweat there. I can answer phones I suppose. I could do some manual work as well. I mean I can press buttons on a feckin' machine. They wouldn't give me me job back where I was workin'. They didn't even tell me I was sacked. They never sent me a P45, never sent me me cards, never sent me nothin'. I was just bleedin' sacked, just sacked. They didn't even offer me a different job than the one I was doin' before the crash. No one wants to give me a job in a wheelchair. I don't know why - just bleedin' third class citizens; worse than women. Women are second class citizens. I've every sympathy with women in this world. They get treated like shit and we people in wheelchairs get treated like bleedin' manure; worst, the bottom of the barrel.

'I try to hoover once a week and I hoover on me knees'

Eight of the women in the study had withdrawn from the labour force when they were in their twenties or thirties to concentrate on home-making and rearing their children. The seven women with multiple sclerosis had all left work before being diagnosed as having the disease. Dolores, who suffered a spinal cord injury when she was eighteen, had married shortly after this and had not been interested in returning to outside employment until her children had left home. Because of their circumstances, these women tended to concentrate far more on the extent to which their domestic labour rather than their outside employment had been affected by their disabilities.

All eight women said that their disabilities caused

problems for them in trying to do housework. Those with multiple sclerosis felt that one of the most threatening aspects of their disease was the way it kept eating into their abilities to do their household chores. For example, Ger said:

> Eight years ago when I was getting bad and I'd be trying to make pastry, I remember standing in the kitchen saying to God, 'Why are you doing this to me? Can't you see that I have four children that needs me?' I remember saying that many a time and I'd be trying to do a thing and it was beating me and I was still holding on and I wouldn't let it beat me. I want to stay doing me housework. That's very important, very important.

The group was equally divided between those who were able to do a good deal of housework and those who said that their abilities to do this were negligible. The four who said they were able to do housework stressed that they took considerably longer than normal to complete household jobs. Debbie also stressed that there were many tasks which she could no longer complete herself and that she had had to give up some of the more enjoyable aspects of housekeeping since her condition had deteriorated:

> By the time my husband comes home the meal is nearly on the table. He doesn't see me having to do the chores. They're not very bad chores but they take longer than they used to, I'll say that, but they are done by the time he comes home. I reckon you ought to have a meal for your husband when he comes home in the evening. I can't stand to stir or make nice sauces or that kind of thing. I drive to the butcher's and he comes out to me in the car and I get what I want. I get things delivered like some meat and supermarket stuff that you can just see and buy. And my

husband does a fair amount. You know, he thinks he does all the shopping on a Saturday; but the boring things I get, the boring things I couldn't ask him to get and he gets the nice things on a Saturday morning.

All the others, like Debbie, pointed out that they often had to adopt rather unorthodox approaches to particular tasks. For example, Dolores said:

I try to hoover once a week and I hoover on me knees. I have pads that I put on me and I'm able to hoover the stairs and upstairs. I put them on me knees and I'm able to hoover for hours and hours. It takes a long time to get through it but how and ever I get through it.

These women stressed that they often had problems in doing household tasks which involved going beyond the confines of the house itself. Elaine, who had multiple sclerosis and did not use a wheelchair, said that she found this quite trying:

To walk I cannot. If they were giving out £5 notes at the far side of that road, I couldn't get over to it. I couldn't and that's fairly concrete. We have three shops around the back road there. Every morning at nine o' clock I used to be around there and I still had MS but now I can't. That to me shows it's getting worse. It is getting a little bit worse. I'm not complaining now, don't think that. Of course I don't go to the supermarket any more. I used to love going on a Friday but now I find I can't walk around it. My husband does the shopping. I write out the list and he goes and gets it. I would like to be able to be doing that again, just pottering around, just seeing what new jazz is out – new things for cleaning saucepans or something. But when he goes he just sticks to the list and that's that. I'd like to be able to look. I would dearly like to be able to go into O'Connell Street on the bus like I used to but I can't do that any more.

All four women who said that they were unable to do household work had multiple sclerosis. Each of them said that they had found it very hard to cope with having to give up almost all their previous housework. Anne, for example, spoke of how frustrating it was to have to look at unfinished chores without being able to do much about them:

> I was so thorough-going in the house and what gets me down is the house. It doesn't now but it did in the beginning seeing little things like dust and the pot wouldn't be where it should be, the floor cloth thrown there but now it doesn't bother me cos I can't let it bother me. I'll tell you what I can do. Me gas stove, me front, the knobs. I can pull off the knobs and I'm getting the vim and I'm going around getting all the splashes off them. Me poor sister; she's here with me all day. I don't expect her to do that much. I mean, she's sixty-two. I'm sure she does be sayin' to herself, 'That feckin' ould bitch, cleaning her stove; what does she think I am?' They don't mind. If I want to do it they like to see me getting and doing it. But regarding keeping a house – I still have a bit up here. I'm able to manage me money.

Both Deirdre and Helen said that they had had to give up control of household finances as well as actual physical housework because of the effects of their disease. Each of them said that this should have meant that they would have a lot of extra time in hand. However, as Helen pointed out, the time which was freed up was badly needed as it could now take so much longer to do basic things like washing and dressing:

I'm not able to do many things now out in the kitchen. Like
I can peel potatoes and things like that but to boil a kettle to
put on the potatoes, it would be too dangerous in the first
place. My husband does all the shopping. I really don't know
the price of anything. I never had it as good, I'm telling you.
I really believe that MS does slow up the thinking. As Jimmy
used to say to me at the beginning, 'There's one thing,
Helen, you don't forget to ask for your wages.' Now I don't
do anything like that. And then there's times when you're as
sharp as a blade. For that again you're in the twilight zone,
you don't know what has happened ten minutes ago.

The fatigue that comes with this thing is indescribable.
It's like a car running out of petrol and you're only hoping
you'll make it to the next garage. You never know what way
you're going to be. Like I could get up say one morning and
it would take me two hours, and that's not counting a
shower, for to get in there and wash myself and dress myself.
I don't want anyone to do any of this for me and I'll have a
little rest between putting on a top, taking off something or
putting back on something. For that again, I could be in and
out in an hour. That's how rapid MS is. You can't be sure of
it from one hour to another.

All four women who were no longer able to do much
housework were among those who went to day centres on
at least one day each week. Deirdre was the only one who
did not enjoy going to the centre. The others, like Carmel,
welcomed the opportunity of getting out of the house and
meeting people:

I can't do any housework really. I go out there and sit beside
Mammy when she's doing it. I can't even cut a piece of meat
or that with me hands but I maybe butter the bread. I can't
do much. Mostly just sitting here with Mammy and chatting.
I do like the Centre cos it takes me out of the house and it

takes me away from things, you know. I can forget all the worry when I'm up there for a few hours. It's great fun. I do have a bit of crack.

Three of the eight women who had opted out of employment to be at home with their children said that they would certainly have an interest in returning to work. However, none of them felt that this was really an option given the extent of their disability. Debbie was upset about this as she felt that her life was now diverging quite a bit from her earlier plans and from the lives of her friends:

I have always been fond of children. You know, I did work with them before I was married. You see that's the sort of thing I would like to have gone back to. But I can't because you would have to be able to move around. I spent the first half of my married life rearing the children; then I was going to do my own things. So many friends do so much more because they are able to and they are at a time when their children are grown up and that's when they can do things, go back to work if they want to. That's just when I can't.

'I think they could have leaned a bit more my way'

The National Rehabilitation Board is a semi-state body with responsibilities in the areas of vocational assessment and placement of people with disabilities in Ireland. It was established in 1967 and replaced the National Organisation for Rehabilitation which had been in existence since the late 1950s.

Seventeen of the thirty people in this study said that they had had at least some contact with the NRB during their lives. Only two of those with multiple sclerosis said that they had any contact with the Board. This contrasted quite sharply with the experience of those with cerebral palsy and spinal cord injury where the corresponding numbers were seven and eight respectively.

The extent of the contact which these seventeen people had with the NRB varied a good deal. Some had received a considerable amount of assistance and were in close touch with NRB staff over a long period. Al, who had set up his own metalwork business after being injured in a car crash, was one of these:

> The NRB are very helpful all right; there's no mistake about that. They got me set up here. They organised to get me into this place, organised to get me to see certain people, organised contracts. But now that they've done their bit, I have to do the rest myself. I don't know if I'm being petty or not but I think they could have leaned a bit more my way insofar as more help was concerned but maybe I had it too easy at the start. I should have been out there myself – doing more work insofar as marketing was concerned.

In contrast, there were people who said that they had very little contact with the NRB. Danny, who had received a substantial compensation award after being injured in an accident, was among these:

> Well, you see, it's sort of an ongoing thing; you're on their files and every now and then they root out the file and say, 'Jasus, there's yer man; what's he doing? Let's look him up. Ah, he's doing nothing. I'd better find him something to do or I'll be in trouble.' That's the way they do it, I think. I've

seen the fella from the NRB four times in the last four years. But I've never gone lookin' for him. He's come lookin' for me. Then again, I'm different from another disabled person; I wasn't looking for a job. They were looking for me to do something, not me wanting to do something.

Seven of the seventeen who had had contact with the NRB felt that it had provided them with a good service. For example, Brian, who had cerebral palsy and who had recently set up a small woodwork business, said that the NRB had been instrumental in getting him started:

> When I was looking for a job outside, I went to the NRB but to no avail. I think that taught me the lesson that segregation exists in Ireland on a very wide basis. Now, I know I got no job but as I say I am taking another leaf out of the book. The NRB suggested that I would try woodwork. Until that moment I had never done it but I said I would give it a try. They organised and paid for a man to come and teach me. They really helped in that way. I hope to be able to be in a contributable position to pay into the running of the house here but I will not in any one year become a JR Ewing from it.

Three people said that their contact with the NRB was so limited that they were not really in a position to say very much about the quality of the service which they had received. Hugh, who had returned to his previous employment after his accident, was among these:

> All I can say is I'm registered with them and I didn't even know I was. Shortly after I went back to work, a fella out of the NRB arrived at the job talking to me. It was only then I discovered I was registered with them. It must have been through the hospital.

The NRB was criticised by seven of those who had had contact with it. All of these were strongly oriented towards open employment and argued that the NRB had done little or nothing to help them. For example, Paul, who had cerebral palsy, said:

> The NRB is hopeless. It's hard to say if they are trying to help me to find employment. They say they are and you ring up month after month to see what the story is and you still get the same answer. It's disheartening. You don't know whether to believe them or not.

Peter, who also had cerebral palsy, got quite angry at even the barest mention of the NRB as he felt that it served the interests of its predominantly able-bodied staff more than those of its clients with disabilities:

> The NRB has sinned because they are promoting the image that they have a kind of expertise in regard to the disabled. I find, frankly, that they are creating a dependency on themselves that they accuse others of doing. I've found many a case where there's a kind of ego trip among social workers and more so in the NRB than anywhere else. They're supposed to be making you independent but they make the 'phone calls and they set up the deals for you – that usually come to nothing. There's the 'phone. I've got a 'phone at home and the obvious thing to do is to say, 'Here, look, mate, do it yourself, we're not going to spoon feed you.' But they don't and they have a very good reason for it in their own light. They could actually do themselves out of a job.

Summary

The relationship between employment and significant physical disability is complex. It raises highly sensitive issues about personal identity and about who is expected, and who is given the opportunity, to contribute to the economy.

The employment circumstances of the group as a whole were very varied. Five were in some form of open employment; four were self-employed; eight were in some form of special training or employment; seven were homemakers; and six defined themselves as unemployed and seeking work.

The group was equally divided between those who were strongly oriented towards open employment and those who were not. The former stressed the importance of what they termed 'proper' employment and were strongly opposed to going into sheltered or special provision for people with disabilities. They stressed that it was very difficult to secure 'proper' work but quite easy to get a special or sheltered place.

Most of those who were actually in sheltered provision enjoyed the work they were doing and the company of their work mates. They seemed quite oblivious to the distinction between open and sheltered provision which was such an issue for others in the study.

It emerged quite clearly that educational qualifications were important in terms of opening up employment options. In fact, it seemed that level of education was more important than severity of disability when it came to employment. However, it must be stressed that possessing educational qualifications did not guarantee employment. Those who could not secure work in spite of having solid qualifications said that they found this to be highly frustrating.

Eight of the twelve women in the study had experience of being full-time home-makers since becoming disabled. Those with multiple sclerosis, in particular, stressed that their condition had impacted very significantly on their ability to do their housework. Most found this very difficult and pointed out that they did not want to be exempt from doing household chores – they saw this as an indication that their condition was deteriorating.

Seventeen of the thirty people interviewed said that they had had at least some contact with the National Rehabilitation Board which has responsibilities in the areas of vocational assessment and training. Some were satisfied with the service they received. Others, however, especially people who were seeking open employment, were very disappointed with it.

CHAPTER 5

INCOME

'Health is wealth' is an everyday saying in Irish life. This reflects the widespread belief that being fit and able is probably more important than anything else. However, it could also be construed as meaning that the healthy and able-bodied have a better chance than the sick and disabled of becoming wealthy. What about the more pessimistic view that sickness and disability is poverty? Or, indeed, the idea that money can never compensate a person for the loss of physical or mental function?

This chapter looks at the financial circumstances of the thirty participants in the study and at how they perceived the role of money in their lives. It is built around four main groups: seven who were earning their income from being employed; two who were living off compensation awards; eight who were dependent on their spouses' income from employment; thirteen who were dependent on state allowances.

'I think it's the "poor disabled" thing again'

We saw in the last chapter that many of the people in the study placed great emphasis on open employment. They saw

102

this as a way of achieving financial independence and a sense of being a contributor to society. How then did those who were in employment fare out financially?

The seven people who were earning their income from employment included two with cerebral palsy, one with multiple sclerosis and four who were disabled due to spinal cord injuries. All seven said that they felt relatively well off compared to many people with physical disabilities. Gerry, who was self-employed, stressed this point but also made it clear that his relative success was due in large measure to hard work on his part:

> I appreciate that the problems of a disabled person in a sheltered workshop who has to go home in a Cheshire Home bus every day are a world apart from the problems I face. None of them could aspire to the level of socialisation, activity, involvement, glamour – for want of a better label – that I enjoy. I make no apology about this. I never worked as hard in all my life as I did for the first three years after my accident. I really worked hard. It hurt like hell and in many ways my wife says to me, 'You're a lazy bastard.' I suppose in certain ways I am; but in the scheme of disability I'm doing very nicely thank you. I hope I haven't become complacent. Whatever we have in terms of material wealth my wife and I have made from a zero base.

Hugh was the only one of the seven who felt that he had not suffered very much financially as a result of being disabled. He attributed this to the fact that his employers had held a job open for him after his accident:

> I wouldn't say I suffered a lot financially really as a result of the accident. I'm on a salary up in the job and you get a yearly rise. That was due in April and I left in March and I

missed it. I was a year behind plus I lost me rank as a manager, which was an extra few shillings. It wasn't until this year that I approached them on it and explained the situation that I had lost money and this year they've made it back up to me. So I'm back now on the right track, sort of thing. For a few years I did lose money. I don't think it was intentional. I think it was an oversight more than anything else with them cos when I did approach them on it they done something. I don't think I'm losing now cos of being in the chair. I'm back on level pegging with everyone else up there.

At the other extreme, Eddie, who had been disabled in a motorcycle accident, was quite adamant that he had lost out very heavily because of his disability and the fact that he had had to change careers. He also stressed that the car which he now needed to get to work and his forthcoming wedding were imposing additional financial burdens on him:

You're working away and you have £150 a week into your hand, or maybe £200, and then suddenly you find yourself with nothing. I went on Disability Benefit. It was only £38 a week or something. And, meanwhile, I was still paying for the bike I hadn't got. It was £65 a month to pay back for three years. It was really hard. Like, if I didn't buy any clothes or shoes I'd have a bit of money. Then I got the job in the civil service. Seventy pounds I come out with after tax, after PRSI, after various union deductions. Me basic is £108. When you think about it – £100 nowadays. I'm trying to get money together to get married and it's nothing. You go out, say you need a pair of shoes, and what are you left with? Like it doesn't last. Compared to now, like I have a car to run; insurance is £1,000.

The two people in this group with cerebral palsy felt that they would have been far better placed to secure more lucrative employment if they had not been disabled. Billy, for example, pointed out that he had only taken his present job, which was offered to him by a friend's father, because he was in desperation after being turned down for other work owing to his disability:

> There was the possibility of a job in a semi-state but they kept me waiting for ten months before they decided it was too much trouble to take me on. The job I have now is part-time and it's not permanent. I'm not paid for holidays or days off. For a full week, I'm paid about £100 but then there's holidays and days off. In the off-season, I go back on DPMA.

None of these people who were in employment said that they were having any major problems meeting their everyday needs. However, all of them felt that other people seemed to think that they had little or no money and that they should spare them from having to pay their way. Paddy stressed that this could be quite frustrating at times:

> Another thing I find is that it is often difficult to pay for things. If I want to buy a round of drinks, or something like that, I have an awful problem convincing people. I think it's the 'poor disabled' thing again. It's a matter of forcing people to let me pay. It's nice to have people paying for you sometimes but it gets a bit much especially when I have the money to pay.

Everyone in this group said that a private telephone and a modest annual holiday were within their financial reach. However, almost all claimed that they faced big problems when it came to making major investments like buying a house. Eddie, for example, who was engaged to be married, described the difficulties which he and his fiancée were having in trying to buy a house:

Where are we going to live? This is the thing you see. I'm only earning £5,000 and Anne is only earning £5,000. Even together, the way the building society works we still haven't enough. Seemingly, there is a scheme for disabled people but you have to be married before they can do anything. So, we were saying that, when we do get married, we'll have to live here, even though you're putting a mother-in-law in with a daughter-in-law and you don't know what hassle that's going to cause. It'll only be for a while, hopefully. If it comes to the stage where we have to get a flat, we'll save bloody hard with a building society. We'll have to do it. We're just taking a chance and see how it goes. We could be living here for a year, two years, three years. We could be living here for six months or six weeks. You don't know.

Hugh was the only one of those who were in employment who was the sole earner in his household. Both Gerry and Paddy's wives were in full-time employment; Eamonn lived with two sisters who were working full-time; and Jane, Billy and Eddie said that their fathers were the main earners in their homes. The fact of not being sole earners in the household certainly took some pressure off these people. Jane, whose father was a wealthy businessman, probably had the least financial worries. However, even her mother stressed that Jane's future was full of uncertainty and insecurity:

She really has a very pleasant life and she is secure financially which is a great thing and she has herself insured financially suppose her health broke down. I mean, the future is a thing you can't think about. I often think if anything happened to us. I mean, the only way that I can figure it out is that she will need plenty of money to help her along her way and, let's face it, it does help. I'd like to see her with everything that she could afford to have help for herself.

But the money doesn't compensate me for anything'

Compensation awards for personal injuries receive much media attention and this can lead to a close association in the public mind between disability and big payments. How then did the people with disabilities in this study fare out in relation to getting compensation?

The only people in the study who gave close consideration to the possibility of pursuing a case for compensation were those who had sustained spinal cord injuries. Those with multiple sclerosis were ruled out because they could not meet the essential requirement of demonstrating that somebody was at fault for their having got the disease. Derek was the only person with cerebral palsy who felt that he might have had a case but said that no one had taken any action about it.

> It was just one of those things, an accident. The doctor made a mistake. He squeezed the forceps too tightly – his first delivery. Nothing was ever done about it.

All ten people with spinal cord injuries had explored the possibility of claiming for compensation following their accidents. However, there were only three cases in which legal proceedings were initiated. Awards were eventually made in each of these. Conor and Danny were awarded substantial amounts of money following court hearings while Dolores received £5,500 in the 1960s in an out-of-court settlement.

These three who received compensation, and especially Danny and Conor, defined themselves as being in a very privileged position compared to other people with disabilities. However, they also stressed that their awards had gone only a small way towards compensating them for the losses which had resulted from their accidents. For example, Danny said:

> I was lucky. I had a good case to start with. It wasn't my fault. They were able to bring up this. I was a real intelligent person and all this stuff. I was stopped in my prime and I'd a great future. I went to the trial everyday and showed them that I've a great brain – it was only my body that was disabled and all this. I had a good crowd of witnesses and good legal people. I'm lucky that I have the money and that I have an independent life. That's what makes me different from most other disabled people. But the money doesn't compensate me for anything. I have no feeling from the shoulders down. Lost the sense of touch – the whole lot.

All three who received compensation awards said that they had been frustrated by the protracted nature of the legal proceedings involved as it meant that they continued to have a very heightened consciousness of the entire circumstances surrounding their accidents for up to six or seven years. However, Conor in particular stressed that the court hearing had been important for him because it gave public recognition to his loss:

> I was offered all sorts of things outside the court. As far as I was concerned, being a hit and run accident, I wanted it to go to court eitherways for one simple reason. Like, if the case was closed outside the court, it's like digging a hole and filling it in again. I was bitter. I was bitter in the early stages of me accident and the way I looked at it after, it wasn't deliberate. As the years went on, I was getting on to myself. I was quite annoyed the way it went on so long – the High Court case. It took five years for it to come up.

Both Conor and Danny stressed that their compensation had enabled them to avoid much of the sense of dependence and loss of opportunity which would otherwise have been inevitable given the extent of their disabilities. Conor had a second source of income, in the form of the social insurance based Disability Benefit, while Danny was dependent on his award alone. Both men identified money as representing a key to their being able to utilise their remaining abilities as it enabled them to secure their own private facilities. Danny was most emphatic on this:

> Well you see, I'm in a very embarrassing position in one way. I've plenty of money. I can't go and complain that I can't get onto a bus in my wheelchair because I have a good car outside the door. I had enough money to buy a car. I can get people to drive that. So, I'm lucky that I have the money and that I have an independent life.

Dolores, who was dependent on Disabled Persons Maintenance Allowance at the time of interview, did not feel that her award of £5,500 in the 1960s had made a particularly significant long-term impact on her life. She expressed regret that she had opted to take a lump sum rather than ongoing weekly payments:

> The case was settled outside the court. It went into the courts that morning and then they were talking. And then in the afternoon they offered me £5,500. It wasn't really a lot when you think of it now. I didn't really understand much about things like that. But there was another offer they made and it would have been a better offer. Me senior counsel didn't think it at the time. It was an offer of so much every week for the rest of me life. I think now it would have been a lot better. With inflation it might have gone up. It was about £10 a week and that was a lot of money in them days.

Sometimes, I think I was mad not to accept that offer. Sure, when I got the £5,500 there wasn't much in it because we got a certain amount to get different things. Then I got the house. It wasn't long going. I got a loan on the house and I'd to pay that back. I hadn't got much left.

All seven people with spinal injuries who had not received compensation felt that such an award would have eased their situation considerably. There was some variation within this group in terms of the extent to which they felt aggrieved by the fact that they had not received awards. The sense of grievance was strongest among five who felt that they had been almost, if not entirely, blameless for their accidents. Eoin was one of these:

> There's people in wheelchairs who get big actions, a few hundred thousand after a few years. I'm not one of them. The insurance people washed their hands of it. Robbed car, you know, and I was a passenger in it. I didn't even know it was robbed. I got a lift, car crashed and I broke me neck and the guy that was driving it only broke his arm. The minute they heard the car was robbed there wasn't a chance.

Neither Hugh nor Kevin, who felt that they had been largely to blame for their accidents, seemed to have any sense of grievance or frustration over their non-receipt of compensation. Hugh, for example, said:

> Me accident was six years today. We're going out celebrating, having a party tonight (laughs). It was a fall, mainly due to me own fault, you know a few jars, trick-acting. We talked about lookin' for compensation. I went to see a solicitor about it. I got a letter back from him and he wanted £10,000 up front to go ahead with the case. If I had £10,000 I wouldn't have

been lookin' for a claim. I don't think I was entitled to anything. It was me own fault. I'd a few jars on me. It was me own fault, nobody else's.

I never really believed that I would get a claim even though I went to see a solicitor. When I talked to him first, he nearly had me believing that I might get something. Then, I got the letter from him about the £10,000. It was going to cost about £200 just to take photographs of where it happened. If there was any chance that I was going to get the claim, he wouldn't have looked for the money. He would have been willing to put up the money himself knowing he was going to get it back in the end. I think he was trying to rip me off, to be honest with you.

Gerry, who had not received compensation, stressed that it was undoubtedly to his physical advantage, at any rate, that he had not got involved in pursuing a claim. He argued that the whole process of fighting for compensation in Ireland means that the injured person's rehabilitation is badly affected when it matters most:

Compensationitis sets in very early and this is where the medics and legal boys are on the horns of a very vicious dilemma. This is because the average legal case in this game takes about three to five years to come to fruition and the lawyer's brief is to maximise, to get ready his client to go in there on the day and do the Christy Brown routine – an Oscar winning performance in front of the jury. That's his brief, to maximise the outcome at the other end with one hundred and fifty or two hundred grand, or whatever it might be.

The medics, on the other hand, will tell you, and they're absolutely right, that unless you bust your gut and work like be-Jasus for the first eighteen months, whatever potential in terms of the physical you have left will not materialise because the system literally winds down and accepts a lower level of expectation. And you have to literally retrain, it's literally like learning to walk all over again; you're a child, you're totally dependent and you've to claw your way back up from that basic level of dependence to a level of independence and that's bloody hard. And that is the dilemma; unless you put it in early on you haven't a hope later on but the lawyers will say, 'Go easy here now cos when you come to court the worse you are the more you're going to get.'

'You get nowhere without money, simple as that'

The relatively low participation rate of married women in the labour force in Ireland means that it is quite commonplace for married women to be dependent on their husbands' income from employment. Married men, on the other hand, have traditionally been the breadwinners and are uneasy about the notion of 'being kept' by their wives. Five women and three men in this study were dependent on their spouses' income from employment. How were they managing financially and what sorts of issues did they raise about this situation?

The financial circumstances of these people ranged from being very comfortable to being very tough and challenging. Debbie, who had multiple sclerosis, made it clear that money was not a problem for her and that she was in the fortunate position of being able to afford a car of her own, help for the house and many material things which enabled her to maximise her independence. One of the prices which she felt she had to pay for this was not seeing very much of her hard-working husband:

I can drive because I've got an automatic car of my own. If I couldn't drive, I'd be in a box. My husband works very hard. He has his own business. He goes very early, at about seven in the morning, which makes a long day. I just wish he could come home comparably early but then with the traffic he doesn't get home until seven so it's a twelve-hour day. He is away a lot as well. I have help for two mornings in the house. It's quite enough for what I want her for. She's good company too. I have a grand little 'phone. It's great. It works through your own 'phone and it's geared for the whole garden which is quite big as you can see. It used to be that I was coming into the house too slow and it would stop when I got there and that was just silly but now I have it all the time in the chair. I'm always get-able or available which is great.

In contrast, both Larry and Eoin said that they were very short of money and that they found it difficult to make ends meet. Larry, who had multiple sclerosis, claimed that his biggest problem was that his wife was both his main carer and the breadwinner for the family. She could only work part-time because of his needs and her earnings were only barely keeping the family going:

> We can't afford to put on the central heating in the winter and we haven't had a holiday in years cos we can't afford that either. Half my life has been cut away by this disease and I suppose I'm only starting to accept now that I can't do things and that there's little point getting frustrated trying to do them. But it's really hard when you can't afford to get out. We can only go out now very occasionally for a drink.

The circumstances of the other five fell between these two extremes but tended towards the lower end of the scale. Carmel, for example, who had multiple sclerosis and who was separated from her husband, described how the added expense of the telephone really stretched her financially:

> Me husband gives me money every Thursday. I didn't have to bring him to court. He gives me £80 and me eldest who's working gives me some as well. I could do with a bit more to pay for things like the 'phone. Me doctor was trying for a 'phone for me now that me husband has left the house. I don't know whether I'll get it. It's very expensive but I need it.

Ger's husband also saw a telephone as being important when there is a person with a disability in the house. However, he said that it was beyond their reach because he had had to cut back on his work when Ger's disease had progressed:

> I can't work rest days and overtime like I'd be able to do under normal circumstances so my earning power is drastically reduced. I have a car outside the door that I can't afford. I never use it except to bring Ger out. That's the only reason it's there. If it wasn't there you could bury her. Also we would like a 'phone but we can't afford it. The 'phone is absolutely and totally out of the question. If I was to get the 'phone in, I would have to get rid of that car.

Elaine, who also had multiple sclerosis and whose husband was a manager in a semi-state body stressed that she was probably much better off financially than many other people with the disease:

> Don't think I'm making meself out big. I mean, we have a car; there are lots of MS patients who haven't got a car. I've got relations in the country. I've only got to lift the 'phone and say, 'Look, I'm feeling tired and fed up.' They'll say,

'Come down' and I can go off. There are lots of MS patients that haven't got the money to do that and it does make a difference, believe me.

None of the women who were dependent on their husbands' income from employment claimed to have any problem with this situation. However, two of the men – Eoin and Kevin – who were dependent on their wives said that they felt very demeaned by this. Both were disabled due to spinal cord injuries and defined themselves as being unemployed – able and willing to work if they could find jobs in what they considered to be a harshly discriminatory society. The two men were very bitter that they had lost their means-tested Disabled Person's Maintenance Allowance when they had got married because their wives' incomes were taken into account. Eoin was only recently married and was finding it particularly hard to come to terms with having to depend on his wife:

> I get nothin' off no one. I just can't believe it. I trusted them and told them I was married. I could have done what loads of people out there are doing and told them nothin' and still collected me money and still let me wife work. But I told them through honesty, being honest and they took all me money off me, stopped everything, two days bleedin' later. She's supposed to keep me. We've gotta pay £16 rent, fuel bills and other things and there's no way my wife can keep me. She can barely keep the two of us going at the moment and they've stopped every penny on me and you're allowed about £10 tax for me and they've stopped about £45 a week now.
>
> The way I think about it, I done me bit for the country workwise and got nothin' back off them. They expect me wife to keep me. It's bad enough that way – it's bad enough not being the breadwinner of the family, being in a

wheelchair makes it even worse. The only thing this government is short of doin' now is throwing us all into a gas chamber and turnin' the feckin' gas on. I'm going back to money all the time. I mean you get nowhere without money, simple as that.

Like Eoin, Kevin was quite adamant that the system of means testing for Disabled Person's Maintenance Allowance needed to be changed:

A disabled pension should be a disabled pension regardless of who else is in the house. If you can't make a few shillings yourself, you're completely dependent on the person you're married to – a burden on them.

'I'm still having me clothes bought for me by me parents who are retired'

People with disabilities have been recognised since the Poor Law era in Ireland as one of the main categories likely to need assistance from the state. The income maintenance system relating to disability has developed quite considerably since the 1930s – or over the life span of the people in the study. For example, the introduction of the means-tested Disabled Person's Maintenance Allowance in 1954 brought a major disability-related scheme out of the area of operation of Home Assistance, which had its origins in the Poor Law scheme of outdoor relief or assistance for 'destitute poor persons permanently disabled from labour by reason of old age, infirmity or bodily or mental defect'.

The period since the 1930s has also seen a growing

emphasis on social insurance schemes. These have as their underlying philosophy the notion that people earn a right to benefits through contributions paid while in employment. The traditional practice in Ireland, as in many other countries, has been to maintain social insurance based payments at a higher level than the means-tested assistance payments.

From 1970 onwards, a number of schemes were introduced which signalled a growing concern to increase the integration and independence of people with disabilities. One of these was a means-tested Mobility Allowance, initiated in 1979, to assist people who cannot walk to make trips away from home. Another was an informal 'Pocket Money' Allowance, for people in long-stay institutions, which has been operated at the discretion of Health Boards since 1983.

What is it like to be on the receiving end of these schemes? What is the quality of life of people with disabilities who are dependent on state allowances? How satisfied are the recipients with the payments they receive?

Thirteen of the thirty people in the study were dependent on state allowances. The majority – eight – of these had cerebral palsy; three had multiple sclerosis and two were disabled due to spinal cord injuries. The greater dependence among those with cerebral palsy can be traced back to their problems in securing employment and to the fact that they were much less likely to be married, and supported by spouses, than those with either of the other disabling conditions.

Anne, who had multiple sclerosis, was the only one of those who were dependent on state allowances who had a history of insurable employment. She had built up an entitlement to Invalidity Pension while the others were dependent on less lucrative means-tested assistance schemes and mainly on the Disabled Person's Maintenance Allowance. Anne said that her pension had been a help in enabling her husband to give up work to be at home with her and that having four incomes coming into the house – albeit three from social welfare – allowed her to have some little extras in her life:

> Jimmy is retired anyway. He was a labourer. He gave up the job because I was here all day on me own and maybe he was foolish but he doesn't think he was. He's fifty-one and he's on the Labour now. The flesh walked off him working and trying to do different things. He'll look for another job and if he gets anything to do that has better hours he'll take it. He gave up because of me really because I was so depressed and then he'd have so much to do when he came home. I get Invalidity Pension because I worked – £37.40 a week. It was hard but it's worth it now. I worked making parts for cars and then I worked as a waitress. Then I got a job cleaning at night but gave that up to get a job early in the morning so that I could mind the kids. I had a great little job. I was on me own cleaning and I could go in as early as I liked. It was a bit spooky sometimes but you had to get over that.
>
> We're getting a little car this evening and that'll be a help. I'll be putting some of me pension towards that. Jimmy is putting in for the medical card. I have a Long Term Illness book. I have to pay for me doctor - £8 - just to look at me. He doesn't spend four minutes with me. He's nice, he's all right. I have to pay for him. I get everything else free - me tablets and vitamins.

Two of those who were dependent on state allowances said that they were suffering severe financial hardship. Paula, who had cerebral palsy and who was living in a nursing home, pointed out that she was not receiving any money – even a Pocket Money Allowance for those in long-term care – directly from the state. She said that she desperately needed money to cover everyday basics but that even her family, with whom she had had a very strained relationship over many years, had refused to help her out:

> The DPMA is given over to the Home and they don't give anything back.   If I was in a Cheshire Home I'd get some money, even £5. Here I don't. At the moment, the social worker is looking into some fund, I don't know what the fund is, to see if they would help me buy clothes. You see, it was okay when I could go up to the house and see Daddy every week and then he'd give me a couple of quid but now I can't go up. I'm after writing to him about four times since I saw you last. I was thinking of getting in touch with those people called ALONE.

Al, who had been disabled in a car accident, felt that his financial difficulties derived from the fact that he was having major problems in launching his new business and that his marriage was in serious trouble. He said that, although he was still receiving DPMA in spite of being in business, he was crippled by his financial circumstances:

> At the moment, I'm getting DPMA for myself, my wife and our six-year-old – £69.50. And, of course, I have a medical card. But that should all stop in April because of the fact that I've started this business. Everyone was expecting me to be on my way to being a millionaire by April which is not the case. I'm up to my eyeballs in debt. There's no way it will stop. At the moment, I'm not getting anything out of the disability cheque. My wife gets the cheque every week. I don't get fed there. I'm at the stage where my wife won't even cook meals for me. I used to get my own meals but my mother wouldn't have that so she decided to send down my meals. I have meals-on-wheels but it's all home cooked. I

don't socialise really. To socialise you have to have money in your pocket. I'm not one to take a drink unless I have money to pay for one back. If I haven't the price of a drink I won't go out; if I haven't the price of two drinks.

None of the others who were dependent on state allowances were as despairing as either Paula or Al. This seemed to be because they all felt that they had some financial back-up available to them, in the short term at any rate, mainly in the form of support from their families. Deirdre, who had multiple sclerosis and who was receiving Widow's Pension, was particularly conscious of the importance of family support:

> The funds are not very good here. See, once you're on Widow's Pension, you don't get a disability grant or anything like that. The kids contribute as much as they can. Now the girl that's getting married, she had to reduce it a bit because her fella wasn't working. Now he's working and they're supposed to be getting married in August and they're trying to buy a house. Then Mary, she was very good when she was working but she's on Assistance now and she can only give £10 which isn't very much in this day and age but how and ever. But me young lad now, he's very good. When he gets a rise I get a rise kind of. So it's really only his wages and me own pension. I'm keeping me fingers crossed cos he's supposed to be let go at the end of August. They don't tell me these kind of things but his sisters were saying that he might be let go. I hope he won't be let go because if he is I don't know what's goin' to happen.

Simon, who had multiple sclerosis and was living in residential care, found it difficult to manage financially but did not regret the fact that he had spent a considerable amount of money on alcohol during his first year or so in the home:

> Financially, it's a struggle. Disability Allowance, it's £35 or £38 and they stop £20 here so you are left with £18. I used to top that up with making stools when me sight was okay and made a fair bit out of that. I'd come close to £40 anyway. They have the OT here and some piece work. I go in there and do a bit of piece work to make ends meet. The money I had coming in here lasted me for about six months. I don't regret drinking it. At the time it was the right thing to do. It just seemed right. I'm not going to regret it. I was able to forget. I was able to get meself out of meself. Going for a drink was getting out of here at the same time. I hate being in here. Again, it's not the place; it's just being stuck in the one spot.

All those who were dependent on state allowances shared the view that they had no option but to live in an eternal present. Peter, who had cerebral palsy and who was living with his elderly parents, spoke out strongly on this and stressed that life on welfare was like a constant balancing act which did not allow for long-term saving:

> Reading, writing, playing guitar, chasing women, drinking, you know. I've a great social life and ironically the social welfare I'm on supports this life but it can't support a long-term thing. If I try saving the social welfare I don't get out and if I go out I can afford a few jars but I can't go in and buy a suit. I'm still having me clothes bought for me by me parents who are retired. I mean I'm forty-four and the Da's retired. You know, what do I do when they die? These things do occur to you, you know, and you have to start thinking in long-term things.

There was little criticism among those who were dependent on state allowances about the levels of payment involved or about the income maintenance system as a whole. Indeed, Christine, who was living in residential care and working in a sheltered situation, said that she was quite happy with the existing provision and that people in residential care should not be over-demanding:

> If you're in a home, you cannot expect the Government to pay for you in a home and then to pay you £20 a week once you're sitting there. It's very costly in these homes without getting £20 on top of that. No way. That's not on. I mean the country is gone very poor really and a lot of people are out of work. I remember when we got nothing when we were in a Cheshire Home and we got nothing when we were in hospital – absolutely nothing. You had to depend on friends if you had them. Granted, I had me mother at home and she gave me a few bob every week. Now that's all changed. We're lucky to be getting our Mobility Allowance. I needn't tell you that makes a big difference to me anyway because I've achieved lots of things through it. I've saved it; put it by and that's how I've got the bits and pieces that I need. I think that £15 in a sheltered workshop is very good because I remember the first sheltered workshop I ever worked in – do you know how much I was getting? Twenty-eight shillings and four pence in old money. We used to laugh about the four pence. We used to say, 'What's the four pence for?'

Most of the dissatisfaction which *was* voiced related to the means-tested Mobility Allowance. Brian, for example, said that this allowance, 'Wasn't worth talking about', and Peter claimed that, 'They want to know what you had for your breakfast when they're deciding whether to give it to you or not.'

The degree of resignation which existed about the welfare system contrasted very sharply with the high levels of dissatisfaction which were expressed by many about their problems in relation to both education and employment. It certainly seemed as if those who had fought so hard, but failed in their search, for employment saw their present financial dependence as the virtually immovable reality which their past efforts had been directed towards avoiding.

Summary

The people in the study talked quite willingly and openly about their financial circumstances and about how they perceived the role of money in their lives.

There was variation within the group as a whole in terms of people's source of income. The main sources were: employment, either their own or their spouses; compensation awards; and state allowances.

All seven who were dependent on income from their own employment said that they felt relatively well off compared to many people with disabilities. They were able to pay their way and afford what they felt were essentials like a private telephone and an annual holiday. They ran into problems, however, when it came to making substantial investments such as buying a house. All but one felt that their earning power had been greatly affected by their disability as the range of jobs open to them was much narrower than would have been the case had they not been disabled.

Three of the thirty people in the study had received compensation awards associated with their disabilities. All three had spinal cord injuries as a result of accidents. Two had received substantial compensation and really stressed the point that they were in a privileged position compared to most other people with disabilities. They argued that, while money could never compensate them for what they had lost, it played a huge role in enabling them to utilise their remaining abilities to the full and to have a good quality of life.

Eight people were dependent on their spouses' income from employment. Their circumstances varied quite considerably and ranged from being comfortable to being very tough. All the men with disabilities who were dependent on their wives' incomes from employment said that they found it very difficult to come to terms with this dependence. The women with disabilities, on the other hand, did not comment on their dependant status and seemed to accept is as being quite 'normal'. One point which was stressed by all who were dependent on their spouses' incomes from employment was that disability has a double-edged impact on family income. It imposes extra costs, on the one hand, while reducing the earning power of the family, on the other.

Thirteen people in the study were dependent on state allowances. Their circumstances varied quite considerably and how they were faring financially seemed to depend very largely on whether they were able to draw on additional financial support from members of their families. However, even those who had family support pointed out that they had difficulty in affording the bare essentials of life. They faced all sorts of problems when it came to meeting what they saw as basic needs in relation to transport, telephone, holidays and clothes.

CHAPTER 6

MARRIAGE

Most people in Ireland marry at some stage during their lives and marriage is widely accepted as being a 'normal' state for those in their adult years. But what of the situation of people who have a significant physical disability? Do they get married like most of the population? Do they experience any particular problems in trying to form relationships and find marriage partners? And furthermore, how do existing marriages respond to either the sudden or insidious onset of disability in one of the partners? These are important questions which do not have straightforward answers. They raise issues about the ways in which we view love, marriage and dependence in our society and also force us to recognise the uniqueness which is associated with the relationships in which all of us, either able-bodied or disabled, may become involved.

This chapter looks firstly at the experiences of people who were single when they became disabled. It then goes on to highlight the various issues raised by those who were already married when they became disabled.

'I'd love to get married'

It is important to remember that any unmarried men or women with disabilities whom we might meet will have had their own particular histories with their disabilities. While some may have had their disabilities all their lives, others may have only recently acquired theirs. Those who have always been disabled will have grown up knowing that their disabilities would be part of the overall package which they would bring to a marriage situation. On the other hand, those who have acquired their disabilities during adulthood will have been forced to make some alterations to their images of themselves as potential marriage partners.

Eighteen people in the study were unmarried when they became disabled. These included all ten with cerebral palsy, six with spinal cord injury and two with multiple sclerosis. In overall terms, the message which came from these thirteen men and five women about relationships and marriage was fairly bleak. However, it also had some very positive aspects, particularly as it related to the experiences of those with spinal cord injuries.

Thirteen of those who were unmarried when they became disabled were still unmarried at the time of interview. The dark side of this is that all these men and women would have liked to marry but felt that this was virtually out of the question for them. The subject of marriage dredged up feelings of tremendous regret and frustration for Paula, who was the oldest person with cerebral palsy:

> Well, I was going with a young man years ago but I decided 'no' when I was so disabled. It wasn't on because twenty years ago – it was more than twenty years ago – it wasn't

recognised for a handicapped person to go with a young man. I rushed out because I wasn't going to be a burden on any man. He said I wasn't a burden and that he wanted to take me and that was it. But I felt I couldn't give him what he would really require and, at that stage, I hadn't come to the stage of maturity, like what I am at now, to know that, 'Yes I could,' because it was a give and take thing. I would advise a girl now, 'If you want to get married, go on and do it as best you can and if you fail then at least you tried. Don't be like me, don't let a fellow pass you by.' That was a very big mistake. No matter how badly disabled, don't let him pass you by. It's a thing you will never, never forget. You will always say, 'Why didn't I do it?' But that 'why' is too late.

Simon, who had multiple sclerosis, had also been close to marrying. However, unlike Paula, he felt that he had been right to turn down the opportunity:

I got engaged once. That was about ten years ago. Now at this stage, it hadn't hit me in the limbs. I ended it. I told the girl the reason why. I said, 'I have MS, it could hit me.' At the same time, at the back of me mind, it wasn't going to hit me. I wouldn't invite anyone into that sort of life. I'm glad now. Imagine it with two or three kids running around and me in a wheelchair. You'd feel twice as bad. I'm just that sort of way. I wouldn't invite anyone into that sort of life. I was walking around. There was absolutely nothing wrong with me except the double vision – bouts of double vision –and now I'm really glad I did it. She wanted to get married. She said, 'It might never hit you,' but I said, 'I'm not willing to take that chance.' I saw her once after by accident. She's married now with three kids, which I'm happy about. We went and had a few drinks and a great conversation. I enjoyed it. She said, 'Well, now you'll let me call in,' and I said, 'No.'

An important point of similarity between the situations of Paula and Simon was that they had both been involved in close relationships in which they were wanted and loved since becoming disabled. Most of the others who were unmarried when they became disabled had not shared this experience. A number of these said that one of the most significant problems which they encountered in trying to develop relationships was that members of the opposite sex tended to treat them as asexual beings who could advise them on their love lives. For example, Peter claimed:

> People seem to look on me as some sort of confessor figure. It was flattering at first but then I realised that it was mostly girls. The girls I thought fancied me, when I fancied them, were only sort of having problems. I am supposed to be solving people's problems. Me, the fount of knowledge and all the rest of it. In a sense, I suppose you could say I had a function then.

Jane, who actively sought to avoid any sexual involvement because of her disability, pointed out that being treated as an 'agony aunt' enabled her to achieve a rather enviable level of closeness to members of the opposite sex:

> I've fancied about one or two men really strongly over the years but, I mean, I've always hidden it very well. I don't believe in letting men kiss me or anything like this. You know, it's only messing. I think it would ruin the friendships that I have because they would probably start saying, 'Oh, she's frustrated in a wheelchair.' It would ruin the fun that I've had and the friendships that I've had. I think that men feel comfortable with me. Certainly, if I go to a booze-up or that all the girls go nuts because they say that the men are all gathered around me, telling me stories and pouring out their hearts.

Billy, who was one of the most disabled people with cerebral palsy, said that one of his main problems in trying to develop relationships with women was that he was generally accompanied by his parents – his helpers – on outings where he might meet potential partners:

> I don't have a girlfriend at the moment and I haven't had many over the years. I find that if I go out it's usually with a group, a family group, and it's a bit difficult to develop a relationship in that sort of situation.

The belief that it is a married man's role to provide for and support his wife and children is part of the traditional culture of Irish society. Although many people would now reject this, it is a notion which is still fairly widespread throughout the country. Certainly, it emerged as being strongly upheld by a number of the unmarried men in this study. In fact, some of these men clearly felt that they were unlikely ever to be in a position to marry because they would not be able to fulfil the role of provider which they saw as being crucial. Peter, a forty-four year old man with cerebral palsy, was one of those who put forward this view:

> I don't get the opportunity to live a mundane life. You know, nine to five. Sometimes I think it would be great: go into work, come home, fall down in front of the telly and have the wife deliver up the dinner. Money is the only thing that's stopping me from marrying. I could fall in love, fall out of love. I know what to do physically and I'm not too worried about my sexual capacity. If I can't do it one way, I can do it in another, you know what I mean. Say what you like, whether you're married or living in sin, you have to have money. One of the girls up the road said, 'What you really need is a woman who is willing to marry and work for you.' Maybe she's right

and maybe she's wrong. But the type of people I'm able to knock around with have no jobs and no money.

Very few of those who were unmarried seemed to see their disability as an insurmountable barrier in itself to the possibility of their ever marrying. One exception to this was Danny, who was one of the most disabled people with spinal cord injuries and who had virtually no financial worries because he had received a substantial compensation award:

> I'd try my chance with any woman but I can't see a woman having an interest in me at all. Who the hell wants a cripple? That's only a general thing, you know what I mean. It's hard to explain. I'm too clever to be a disabled person – no, if I didn't think so deeply into these things, I'd probably be better off. Like thinking into women. So what *do* you think? What does a woman look for in a man? She wants children. She wants other things. I can't supply her with those kind of things. So, it's bad to be thinking about these problems. It gets you down. But I'll try anything with any girl.

Danny's view of his prospects of marrying had once been shared by Eddie, who was also disabled due to a spinal cord injury but happily engaged to be married at the time of interview:

> I'm engaged to be married. I only met the girl after the accident so she didn't know me before the accident. And the girl I had been going out with coming up to the accident, we were supposed to be engaged. She was going to stick with me and all this but I don't know what happened. I sort of cooled off. She used to come in every night; every chance she got she'd come in. But I wasn't the same as what I was. I wasn't the same as I am now. I never thought there'd be

anyone. I wasn't expecting anyone to come along wanting to go out with me, mostly because of the wheelchair. And then I was saying to meself, 'Jasus, I'm not any different. That's just a seat as far as most people are concerned.' So lucky enough my fiancée accepted it that way, that it had no say in what I thought or I wanted or I needed. She enquired into everything about my accident – what I can do, what I can't do, everything. We just realised we were two people right for each other and that was it - no stops, nothing. Ah, Jasus, we were head over heels and it wasn't just, 'Ah, she's a lovely looking girl.' We just sort of hit it off.

It is widely recognised that people with significant physical disabilities are less likely to marry than able-bodied people. The people in this study have certainly pointed to many reasons why this is the case. These include: failure among able-bodied people to recognise and accept the aspirations to marry of many people with disabilities; unwillingness among people with disabilities to burden themselves on marriage partners; and, crucially, the often disadvantaged position of people with disabilities in terms of income, employment, housing, personal care assistance, and transport and access.

'How could she bleedin' resist me?'

What then of those who *do* get married in spite of their disabilities? Is there something exceptional about these people? How do their marriages work out? How do they cope with the sorts of problems which have been identified by those who were unmarried?

A total of just five people had got married after they

became disabled. Three of these were men and two were women. Only one of the five had married someone whom she had known prior to becoming disabled. This was Dolores, who was disabled due to spinal cord injury. She had married her pre-injury boyfriend approximately four years after her accident. The marriage did not work out and ended in a legal separation a few years later. Dolores was very philosophical about the breakdown which she attributed to a number of factors including her young age at marriage, her husband's drinking and her own concern about the fact that she was disabled:

> He started drinking after the accident. We were okay when we weren't married but when we got married I think that's when the trouble started. To him, I was no different from anyone else. He didn't see the chair. He just seen me as a person. I always put that in the way. Now that I go back over it, I probably did put it in the way. I couldn't do things like you for instance. You're a woman and you could do things that I couldn't do. And I used always think like that. I had a bad mind probably. I used to say when he's away maybe he's with someone else, you know the way. I think it did get in the way a lot. I'm not bitter or anything against him, don't get me wrong. I mean there was fault on both sides. I mean, we did know each other but I don't think we gave ourselves a chance. I'm a lot more mature now. I was young.

The marriages of all four who married people they had met only after they had become disabled seemed to be solid. These, like Eddie who was engaged, stressed that both they and their partners had entered the marriage with a clear knowledge and understanding of the fact that their disability would have to be accommodated. All of them also said that they had been forced by sceptical outsiders to go through a process of justifying their decision to marry. Gerry, who was disabled due to spinal cord injury, saw this questioning and disapproval as being yet another dimension of the social challenge facing people with disabilities in Ireland:

> When we were going round together it was unusual but accepted that a disabled person and an able-bodied person might do that. When the option of marriage came into the frame a lot of things changed – attitudes changed. We were faced with convincing a lot of people that what we were doing was: 1. feasible, 2. proper, 3. realistic, 4. viable, and several other things as well. And it was yet another example of 'the struggle'.

Christine, the only person with cerebral palsy who had married, said that the opposition which she had faced to her marriage was almost overwhelming. She said that much of the disapproval about her marrying centred on the issue of sex. However, she felt that this concern was misguided as there is far more to a marriage than sexual intercourse:

> I find, okay, we have our disagreements but I'd miss him if he wasn't around. You might say, 'Oh, I'm browned off. I'm fed up,' but I can't see my life without him and he says the same. Seriously speaking, we both feel the same way. We both live for each other. Okay, we can't have sex or we can't have things we'd like to have. But sex is not the main thing in a marriage. It shouldn't be. It's made the issue nowadays which I think is wrong. That's one of the mistakes of the Church. For instance, as I say, when I went to the local priest, he said if we couldn't have intercourse we couldn't get married – our marriage wouldn't be consummated. That was the answer back to me. I mean, in God's name, God himself wouldn't expect that. You can love each other and enjoy each other and be happy without sex.

Two of the men who had married since becoming disabled were among those who were unemployed and dependent on their wives' income from work. Both argued that their financial dependence imposed a major strain on both themselves and their marriages. Eoin, who was only recently married, felt that his dependence on his wife was chipping away at his determination and self-esteem:

> I was in the wheelchair when I met me wife. How could she bleedin' resist me? Women were never any problem to me. I'd just go over to a woman and give her one of these bleedin' smiles and that would be it. I'd see little hearts in her eyes. The wife treats me like anybody else. She treats me like a guy that's walking down the road. I don't want any concessions from me mot either. I feel lousy. Me mot gives me seven or eight pounds to go and have a drink. I feel like a beggar takin' it off her and she'd make me take it. I do feel very depressed over it sometimes. The wife sayin', 'Don't be gettin' depressed,' and I'm puttin' her into a sort of bad humour which I don't like doin'.

It is hard to say why it was that those five respondents who married after becoming disabled succeeded in achieving this while many others were failing to attain this ambition. Those who were in successful marriages seemed to be more confident than the others and refused to be defined by their disabilities. As Eoin put it, 'I don't come with the wheelchair; it comes with me.'

Those with spinal cord injuries were more likely to get married after the onset of disability than those with cerebral palsy. (It is difficult to make comparisons with the people with multiple sclerosis as most of these were already married when they became disabled.) One reason for this may have been the fact that all those with spinal cord injuries had a number of years' experience of dating before they became disabled. Also, unlike the people with cerebral palsy, they had all lived away from their parents and built up a degree of independence before their accidents. A number of people with cerebral palsy stressed that their parents' ongoing protectiveness towards them tended to keep them in a childlike world which was far removed from that of a marriage situation. Billy was most emphatic on this point:

> It's hard to explain. It's just that living at home can be a bit confining even though my parents are understanding. If I was on my own, if I moved out, everything would depend on me whereas now it doesn't. It's just the fact of being able to make decisions. If you fall flat on your face, it's up to you. I'm twenty-nine now and I think it's high time I thought of it. Perhaps it's because here I feel, even though I can do what I want more or less, to go from here to a marriage situation, I don't know, I feel I would like to get myself straightened out before getting married. To do that I think I would have to move out.

'It takes a good marriage to weather disability'

People may already be married when disability enters their lives. What happens in these cases? Do the marriages survive? What of the marriage vow to support each other in sickness and in health? Does it make any difference if the disability strikes suddenly or comes on gradually?

Twelve of the people in the study were already married when they became disabled. Four (all men) were disabled as a result of spinal cord injuries and eight (seven women and one man) were disabled by multiple sclerosis. All these men and women stressed that their marriages had been severely rocked and affected by the onset of their disability. Some of the marriages fell apart, some were strengthened and certainly none were ever the same again.

Being married when disability strikes can, it seems, be either a blessing or an added burden or indeed a mixture of both. The marriage partner can be a source of tremendous support, the ultimate friend. On the other hand, he or she can be a heartbreaking disappointment who seems to march to a different tune.

There were three cases of marital breakdown and one of severe marital problems among the twelve people who were already married when they became disabled. What lies behind these figures is a sea of hurt, bitterness and human feelings in which the loss of function associated with the disability often seems insignificant compared with the losses associated with the marital breakdown.

Both Conor and Al, who were separated from their wives, stressed that their marriages had been in difficulty before they ever became disabled. The onset of disability in this situation was really the final straw which eventually tipped the balance. Conor, who had been married for about two years before his accident, was particularly emphatic on this:

> Even before me accident – we were getting on okay – but it wasn't really a good marriage. The personal end of it, the sex end of it was zero. I mean as a percent out of a hundred, it was less than five percent. That was before the accident so you can visualise what it was like after the accident. It was no marriage when you think of it. The social life wasn't great. That was there from the word go. There was a squabble

about going for a drink. She wasn't on for going out – just to be around the house the whole time. Socialising with her was really hopeless.

Paddy and Carmel, on the other hand, felt that they had only begun to experience marital difficulties after they had become disabled. In Paddy's case, the problems began when he was still in hospital after his accident. He and his wife were still living together at the time of interview – some twelve years later – in spite of the tension and violence which existed in the relationship:

> When this happened to me, she went to bits. She really went apart and started drinking and all that. So, it's really since the accident. She's grand at times - about ten percent of the time she's okay – very seldom. There are times and she'd say, 'Get out of me sight,' and she'd force the chair into the room. See, there's not a lot you can do about it. She'll lock the door then after you and that's you, you can't do a thing about it. Like what's the use of flattening her or striking her? There's no point in it. She'd bash you round as much as she liked. It's nothing for her to bash the head off me. And then there's not a word about it the next day. So it's an awful mixed up thing.

Carmel, unlike Paddy, was separated from her husband and had not experienced major problems in her marriage until four or five years after becoming disabled. She was suffering from multiple sclerosis and felt that the onset of incontinence had been a major factor which caused her husband to leave her for another woman:

> My husband left me two years ago. He went off with another woman who has three children. If the waterworks hadn'ta went it wouldn't have been half as bad. It's very degrading.

Like, I have disposable sheets for the bed and I have the commode upstairs cos maybe two or three times in the night I have to get up and go to the toilet. But my toilet is downstairs so I have the commode beside the bed. You see, I think he couldn't face up to that. I wouldn't like to put you off marriage. It had its good moments. There was good years. I was married twenty-one years last March.

The onset of disability in one marriage partner cannot but affect the life of the other. This point was made over and over again but was particularly highlighted by Hugh and Ger's partners who took part in the interviews which were held with them. Ger's husband, John, stressed that the couple's whole life had been put under enormous strain by Ger's multiple sclerosis. The worst time for him had been when she began suffering from severe depression:

I used to go up to the lads' bedroom and cry up there. I couldn't cry in front of her but I could see something drastic was happening. I used to go up and sit in their room. You know, you'd think, God give me strength or something like that. Something give me strength to keep with it. I leaned an awful lot on the two boys. They were a tremendous strength to me. They never realised it themselves at the time. They grew up to be men before their time. My work mates offered to work their rest days so that I could stay at home with her. They realised how bad it was. But yet, I couldn't do that meself even though I appreciated what they were at. I felt it was something that the two of us had to beat and last week when she said to you, 'I have beaten it,' they were the sweetest words I have heard out of her mouth for thirteen years. I have been waiting to hear that. And she has beaten it.

Hugh's wife, Mary, said that their marriage had almost broken down in the first few years after Hugh's accident.

She recalled the physical strain as well as the mental turmoil which she herself had suffered in the aftermath of his accident:

> I find it very hard still. I think the fact that I was so young. I was only twenty-two. I could see me whole life gone, shattered. I felt that I would have coped better if he was gone – dead. I'm getting a bit older now and kind of accept it. I was only after getting married, me whole life ahead of me – just gone. He used to come in and swing me up, that's gone, and we used to go for walks, we'd walk anywhere. When he came home from hospital it was much more difficult than I'd expected. I think it was the fact that I had the baby and the two-and-a-half year old. When he came home, it was like having two babies. No one would ever ask how I was. It was always, 'How's your husband; how's the kids?' I even said to me Ma at one stage and sat there and cried that, 'no one gives a damn how I feel and it's me that's doing everything.'

It seemed that the marriages which were affected by spinal injury were more likely to run into major problems than those which had to cope with multiple sclerosis. The main reason for this probably lies in the fact that spinal cord injury has a very sudden and shocking onset compared with the generally more insidious multiple sclerosis. The long hospitalisation which follows a spinal cord injury also means that marriage partners are separated at a time when their lives are in crisis. Lengthy hospital stays are relatively unusual in the early stages of multiple sclerosis and so husbands and wives are not shot out of their normal environment and forced to cope with difficult times in a rather artificial hospital setting. Furthermore, the relatively slow onset and progression of multiple sclerosis gives married couples a better chance to get used to the changes imposed on their lives than does the shattering and dramatic onset of spinal cord injury.

The ways in which married couples cope with the progressive deterioration, the numerous symptoms and the uncertainty of multiple sclerosis are many and varied. Anne and Helen stressed that it is vital that couples continue to see the funny side of life if they are faced with a disease like multiple sclerosis. Helen said that she and her husband, Tim, had enjoyed many a joke while coping with her disability:

> He's marvellous for to be able to cope with me in the first place. I'm not such a nice person to live with at any time. But when anyone says to him, 'God, you're great for to stick her,' just our own friends, 'God, how do you stick her?' I do say, 'I'll tell you how he's able to stick me. When you're going around on crutches and he tells you off or anything, one good blow of a crutch and that puts him back straight. He knows who to be nice to.' We can laugh about it and that's the main thing.

Debbie, who was in her early fifties and who had had multiple sclerosis for twelve years, felt that her husband's pragmatic and sometimes frustrating approach to her condition had been helpful over the years in motivating her to remain involved in her normal day-to-day activities:

> They don't like to think there is anything wrong with you. Husbands don't expect you to do less. I mean they are awfully good for doing an awful lot. In the beginning, I said I couldn't appear in a wheelchair but it's up to you to make the most of it and you can go places if you have to. I couldn't go down the garden if I hadn't got the chair. My husband would say to me, 'Did you see the delphiniums?' and I'd say, 'No.' 'Well go and look at them.' So I mean you do. I often

say to my husband, 'I'm much worse,' and he says, 'Indeed you're not.' And I think, 'If only you could see me half the time.' By the time he gets home, the meal is nearly on the table. But he doesn't see me having to do the chores. They're not very bad chores but they take longer than they used to, I'll say that. But they are done by the time he comes home. I reckon you ought to have a meal for your husband when he comes home in the evening.

'God takes the good and leaves them rotters'

Having a disability does not miraculously exempt a person from having to cope with the death of a husband or wife. Very often there is a tendency to see the person with the disability as the partner who has exclusive rights to all the health problems with which a couple will have to deal. Clearly, this is ridiculous but it is understandable because the partner with the disability will probably have had far more than an average share of hospitalisation and contact with medical personnel.

The people in the study were still relatively young so it was not surprising that only a couple raised the issue of their spouses' deaths. However, what they said pointed to the fact that losing a partner can represent a double blow for a person with a disability as it may involve the loss of a virtually indispensable carer as well as that of a friend, companion and lover. Ger, who had multiple sclerosis and who was very dependent on her husband, was one of those who talked of widowhood. Her anxiety about the possibility of losing her husband was very intense:

He's the only one that will get me out of depression. It doesn't matter who I talk to around here, I have to come back and tell him, talk to him. He's the only one that is able to get me out of that depression. Isn't that awful and I shouldn't be burdening him. But that's why I have to look after him now. I do pray that he won't be taken before me. I'm a very hard person to live with and he has to put up with me and things have to be perfect for me. I'm afraid that he'll go before me. See, I have a very active mind. It's extremely active and you see it runs away on me and I do be sitting and thinking and thinking.

Deirdre, who also had multiple sclerosis, was the only person in the study who had already been widowed. She was a sad and lonely woman who talked lovingly of her husband who had died suddenly nine years previously:

He was only fifty when he died. He was the best husband that ever lived. He was great and I do often ask why God takes the good and leaves them rotters. I liked dancing and the pictures and that. I used to go into the pictures with him, the Lord have mercy on him. Might just walk around town and go in for an ice-cream or a coffee. And he loved standing for hours looking at tools in a window. He was the kind that liked to do things himself in his own time. He built the kitchen out the back for me. He used to make little dishes and that as well. He worked on shift work and when he'd come home he'd do the washing and that for the kids. He was great. He was awful good.

Summary

The whole subject of marriage and personal relationships is a very delicate and emotive one in our society. It involves the issue of sexuality which people often have great difficulty talking about especially where it involves people with significant disabilities. The participants in the study had a good deal to say about their feelings and experiences in relation to marriage and it was clear that they saw it as one of the most significant institutions in Irish life.

Eighteen of the people in the study were single when they became disabled and five of these had married since. All those who had remained single said that they would have liked to marry but felt that this was most unlikely for a range of reasons including: the fact that they tended to be treated as asexual beings; their unwillingness to be a burden on a marriage partner; and their disadvantaged position in relation to employment, income, housing, personal care assistance, transport and access.

Those who had been disabled all their lives seemed to have far more difficulty in forming and maintaining personal relationships than those who had acquired their disabilities later in life. Only one of the ten people with cerebral palsy had married. All the others who had married since becoming disabled had spinal cord injuries. Only one person had married someone she had known prior to becoming disabled. This marriage broke down after a few years. Those who had married people they had met since becoming disabled said that the relationships were working out well in spite of the added dimension of their disabilities.

Twelve of the people in the study were already married when they became disabled and they all stressed that disability had imposed huge strains on their marriages. Three of the marriages had broken down and another had been in serious difficulties since the onset of disability twelve years earlier. Marriages involving people with spinal cord injuries seemed to be more vulnerable than those involving people with multiple sclerosis.

Those whose marriages had survived stressed that they had really had to work at the relationships since the onset of their disabilities. Good communication, positive thinking and a shared sense of humour were identified as being crucial in relation to keeping the marriages alive.

Only one of the thirty people in the study had been widowed. However, her experience, coupled with the views of some of the others, highlighted the point that the death of a spouse for people with significant disabilities can involve the shattering loss all at once of a friend, lover, breadwinner and principal carer.

CHAPTER 7

RESIDENCE AND PERSONAL CARE

We live in a society in which there is great emphasis on privacy and especially the privacy of our bodies. From a very early age children are taught and encouraged to be fully independent in relation to personal care activities like eating, toileting, washing and dressing themselves. Having a disabling condition can mean that this independence is either never achieved or is gradually or suddenly taken away. A level of dependence can in turn raise all sorts of issues in relation to the provision of care and housing. This chapter seeks to explore these issues through the experiences of the thirty people with disabilities and some of those who were involved with them.

'Jesus, you'd want to be a sound man that it wouldn't drive you mad'

Defining a physically disabled person's level of independence in relation to personal care may seem to be quite easy at first. However, the participants in this study made it quite clear

145

that this whole matter has a number of dimensions which are often not very apparent. Firstly, a person's level of independence may well depend just as much on available facilities and technology as on degree of physical function. Secondly, levels of dependence and independence are not necessarily fixed but may vary very considerably even from one hour to the next for people with changeable conditions like multiple sclerosis. Thirdly, the social atmosphere and prevailing attitudes surrounding a person may impact very significantly on their abilities to function independently.

The thirty people with disabilities in the study were more or less equally divided between those who said that they were essentially independent in relation to personal care and those who said that they needed assistance with activities like dressing, washing, eating, toileting and getting in and out of bed. Almost all those who said they were independent stressed how fortunate they felt about this. Debbie, who had multiple sclerosis, was among these but she did not conceal her frustration at the decline in her overall level of ability:

> Funny how you can get by. I can do big things. I can drive and change gears. I don't have to change gears in the automatic car and my right leg is okay. It's the little things that are difficult. I know a girl who is very much worse than me. She is in a chair all the time and she can't walk. She can't feed herself and she has to have help to dress. See, I am lucky, I suppose. I don't need that kind of help. I don't really. It just annoys me that I can't do much. I would love to be out cutting the grass. I can only weed the edges where I can reach. I have always done things and how I would love to still be able to play tennis.

Seven of the ten people disabled due to spinal cord injury said that they were independent in relation to personal care. However, they stressed that it had taken a considerable amount of time and effort to regain their independence after their accidents. For example, Hugh said:

> At the beginning it was tough. I couldn't do anything. I couldn't do anything. I'd no strength in me arms like I have now. I'm very lucky in that I have full use of the top half; I have full use of my arms. When I was in hospital, one of the most difficult things – it's not difficult now – was dressing yourself. I picked that up in hospital. I wasn't going to ask for help from anybody. I always wanted to try meself first no matter what it was. I was so weak when I came home but I was determined. Jenny had to do everything. I couldn't get in and out of the bath or use the toilet myself. Now I can do all those things. I go out and get the coal. I'm not saying I do it a lot but I can hoover the place and them sort of things. The first year or two was really very tough.

Each of those who said that they were independent in relation to personal care activities mentioned that they tended to take considerably longer than normal to perform these. This was particularly true of the five people with multiple sclerosis and Eamonn was one of these:

> What happens to me, I'm up and down the stairs like a yo-yo and some evenings when I get to bed I feel like I want to go to the toilet so I get out and nothing and I get back into bed and as soon as I get back into bed I want to go again. Jesus, you'd want to be a sound man that it wouldn't drive you mad. Sometimes I get out to shave and I feel dizzy and I'm hardly able to put the shaving soap to my face but you just have to fight, you have to do it. You get over it. Put your mind on something else, make sure you wouldn't cut yourself too much or something – cut your throat in the meantime!
> I must do everything very slowly. If I rushed up the stairs

I was gone. The Doc taught me that because when I'd be getting out of bed I'd just throw over the clothes and get out of the bed and I'd feel 'Ooh!' Don't go in head first, like. So you take everything very easy. It does help you. You have to fight. You'd be walking down the stairs, sometimes you'd get back into bed and say, 'I have to get down those stairs.' So I might walk down a few stairs and sit down and I'd walk down the rest of them and I'd get there. Then I'd be saying, 'How are you going to get back up them again?' You know, you manage. I always like to have people around because I'm always afraid that I'm going to drop or something.

Peter, who had cerebral palsy, also stressed that he was quite independent as long as he was left to do things his way:

No physical assistance for going to bed, going to the loo, eating, going out. You saw me getting on to the bus. As a matter of fact, most of the physical assistance offered by people usually throws me out of kilter. I have a plan which works. It goes clickedy-click until someone interferes and tries to help. But they are well-meaning and I don't object to them. I might as well let them do it. Better than a poke in the eye!

Some of those who were independent in relation to personal care said that toileting still remained a highly problematical aspect of their lives. For example, Al said:

Not being able to go to the loo properly is one of the biggest, I found anyway, hitches. In my position, I'm going around wearing this bag on my leg. You're worrying that something might happen and you're worrying, say you might empty it and forget to close it, and next thing somebody would say, 'Excuse me, but, eh, I think there's something wrong here.' That would be an embarrassing situation. Or there again, I've to take pills for bowel movement. These pills normally take eight hours to work but sometimes they can work in four and you could be outside your own home and that's when one really wants to jump off a cliff. It's really embarrassing sometimes. Not that it happens too often; it only happened me, I think, once and you'd make sure it didn't happen again.

Eoin pointed out that his problems in relation to toileting were really aggravated by the fact that so few toilets in public places are accessible to people using wheelchairs:

I always say, 'I don't come with the wheelchair, it comes with me.' I've only about 40 percent use of me hands at the moment but I can do sort of 99.5 percent or 99.75 percent for meself. I wear a bag for urine which I don't like doing. Sometimes I don't wear it. I know when I'm going to the toilet sort of both ways so if I'm staying in I don't wear it and if I'm going out I'll wear it. When you go out, if I'm going down the road and I feel like going to the toilet where am I going to go? There's very few places where you can go in and get into the toilet. If you're in a pub you might be okay if you can get at the toilet. If you're just wheelin' somewhere and you feel like going to the toilet – I mean, you can hold it for so long but not very long especially in a wheelchair. People walking around could hold it a hundred times longer than me. Another thing about going up the road, there's no way you're going to jump into a field especially if you're on your tod wheelin' up the road. I make sure everything's sort of okay before I venture out.

There was enormous variation in the range of abilities among those who said that they were dependent in relation to personal care. Helen, who had multiple sclerosis was one of the least dependent:

I must say, 'thank you,' to the man above for leaving me with my hands. I think that would be the worst thing that could happen to not be able to use my hands for washing myself and things like that. It can be a very degrading illness. I know what can happen and what might happen to me but I'm so thankful that it hasn't come to that. I can manage most things myself. It would only be the odd day now I wouldn't be good. Then, it could take me hours to get washed and dressed. Nearly everyday I have to get me home help to put on me tights and shoes. I'm incontinent but there again I have the toilet and as soon as I get that little bell that says, 'water on the brain', I just get moving and it's quite handy in there. It's terrible, really. You say to yourself, 'How am I going to manage?' and especially if you know there's no way of getting to a toilet, no possible way of getting to a toilet. So you just have to go out in the hope and pad yourself very well and more times out of ten you come home all right, a bit damp but okay.

At the other extreme, Danny, who had been disabled in a car crash, was one of the most dependent:

I haven't got the use of me hands or the inside of me – sexual organs, stomach or anything like that – doesn't work. I have no feeling from the shoulders down. Lost the sense of touch, the whole lot. When I'm in bed I can't do anything. I can't read the paper or read a book or anything cos I can't use my hands. I need someone to help me. I can't even feed meself. Now sitting up I can put a strap on me and feed meself. I can use remote control and turn on the telly. I can read the paper, I can read a book. I can put a biro in my hand, I can write. I can put a nail on my hand and type on a typewriter. So sitting up is grand. Lying down I can't do anything. The way I look at it is, you look on the bright side of it. It's very hard to see the bright side of it. It's very hard. I'll tell you, night-time is the worst when I'm in bed and you're thinking or you wake up early in the morning and you have to lie there until someone comes and gets you up.

All those who needed assistance with personal care tended to see what are often taken-for-granted activities, like going to the toilet, as a series of many different tasks demanding a whole range of skills. Anne, who had multiple sclerosis, was typical of these:

> I can get out of the chair and on to the loo cos I have a bar in the loo. They pull me pants down for me and I manoeuvre on to the loo. I have to have a commode in the bedroom. I haven't got much movement – this side of me – you know. I have no power in me legs at all. I can stand up but I find now in the last few months that I'm not able to stand that well. I suppose, it could be a lot worse. I'm washed down in front of the fire. Everyone goes out and me husband locks the whole house up and I have me wash in front of the fire. I only wipe meself down during the week and he washes bottom, top and tail. I can wash me face and I can comb me hair but I can't dress meself. I get so tired, I get exhausted. Me husband used to say, 'A drop of whiskey would do you good.' But, as I say, I'm drunk before I start, kinda giddy, you know.

There was a sense of striving among all those who had problems with personal care to be as independent as possible. Brian, who had cerebral palsy, was particularly keen to work out ways of being able to manage himself:

> I try to minimise the amount of help I need. Thank God, I have been successful in doing so. Feeding – basically, I need no help. All I need in dressing is my buttons fastened and so on. Now recently, I have bought boots which zip up rather than laced shoes so again I am cutting the disabledness out of dressing. Now, the bath is a bit difficult. It is upstairs and

secondly, the actual getting in and out is quite a job. But again, I can do that partly on my own and if I need assistance I know it's there. But basically, the shower is always on for me. I have hand rails when needed and I also have a bench in the shower and I do use one of the kitchen chairs to sit on before and after a shower.

Paula, who also had cerebral palsy and who was living in a nursing home, expressed a lot of frustration over the way in which she felt that her limited independence had been even further curtailed by the way things were organised within the home:

> I can write all on my own. I can turn pages on my own. I can hold a book on my own. I can eat on my own, provided I have a table high enough and that it won't move. I can brush my hair on my own. I have to be dressed, undressed and toileted. You don't have a chance to do things here at the nursing home. This is what annoys me. I would wash my own clothes at home but you can't do that here so it throws you back. What you have learned to do is taken away from you.

The fact that dependence can be created by social attitudes and unexamined routines was also highlighted by Paul's mother, who felt now that she had always tended to do too much for him since he was a baby with cerebral palsy:

> His sister is better with him than I am because I did everything for him – toilet, dressed him. And on one occasion when I was in hospital, there a few years ago, she put him straight. She said, 'Mam's not here now. I won't do, I can't do what she did for you and you'll have to just pull up your socks or else ...' And when I came home he was going to the toilet himself, fixing himself, making his bed, dressing himself and the only thing I have to do now is fasten

his laces and buttons. That's all. I don't think it's laziness with him. It was something to do with the brain. I don't know but he could be lazy too. They feel everything is being done.

LIVING IN THE COMMUNITY

Mobility problems and needing help with personal care and indeed other activities of daily living like cooking, house cleaning and doing the laundry tend not to be associated in the Irish mind with 'people in their prime'. So, what happens when they are part of the equation? How do people with significant physical disabilities manage when it comes to meeting their housing and personal care needs?

Twenty-six of the thirty people in this study were living in the community and four were in residential care settings. This section will deal with the experiences of those living in the community and the issues relating to residential care will be explored later.

'I'd really prefer if they'd all leave the house so I can organise an orgy for myself – get rid of them for God's sake'

Dolores, who was disabled due to a spinal injury, was the only person based in the community who lived alone. The other twenty-five lived with either their parents, siblings, spouses, children or some combination of these. Parents featured very strongly in the living arrangements of those with cerebral palsy. In fact, all seven who remained in the community were still living with their parents in spite of the fact that they ranged in age from twenty-eight to forty-three years. Each of these had seen at least one brother or sister move away from home and three said that they were now living alone with their parents. Derek, who was very dependent in relation to personal care, found that living with his elderly parents was imposing an intolerable strain on everyone concerned:

> So what's in the future is a Cheshire Home – as soon as someone dies and there's a bed free. If I stay at home, Da or Ma is going to lift me one day and one of them is going to drop dead and I don't feel like living with that. So in that way, I have no alternative. I happen to have a conscience.

Brian's mother said that he did not need much physical assistance but that his moods and very presence in the house had imposed considerable strain over the years:

> But now I had hard times with him, with tantrums and that, you know. He used to go into them very often and it was causing terrible tension in the home. Terrible tension it used to cause and his brother said to him, 'All right, if it continues, I'll have to move out cos I couldn't stick the likes of that.' So he sort of cooled down after that. I suppose he was about thirty then. That was two or three years ago. The tantrums would be over different things. Like, he'd start a row over nothing and he'd up-end a table or anything that was there. Used to lift it and he put a table through a glass door one night, arguing with his father over nothing. It was all unnecessary. See, they are a handful in their own way but I argue that you own them. What can you do? There's no one else going to rear them. You just have to put up with it. That's how I look at it.

There was a consensus among the parents of those with cerebral palsy that their non-disabled children had suffered because of the level of attention which tended to be directed towards the child with the disability. For example, Jane's mother said:

> It had a dreadful effect on her sister, Susie. Nobody ever thought to ask how she was and she grew up fighting. She had to fight for her place in life. People didn't think. It was all Jane. It's only now I see how nice Susie is. She married a lovely fellow and it's unbelievable to see because she has somebody she knows cares about her and I didn't get on with her very well. Didn't get on with her because I suppose the root of the whole problem was Jane. I was always looking after her and then you see there'd be rows and rows. But now we are tremendous friends, now that she knows she has someone else. But having a handicapped child in the family does affect the other children.

The parental home, which was so crucial for those with cerebral palsy, played a much less significant role in the ongoing lives of those with either multiple sclerosis or spinal cord injury. The 'marital home' – consisting of spouse and/ or offspring – tended to be far more important for these. This was particularly true in the case of those with multiple sclerosis. Eight of these were living with their marriage partners and/or some or all their children. In contrast to those with cerebral palsy, none of these were living with anyone who belonged to an older generation than their own. Deirdre, who was fifty-one, widowed and living with two daughters in their twenties, was quick to point out that having multiple sclerosis had upset the balance between the generations in her life. She said that she felt older than her own mother and that her daughter had had to grow up before her time:

> My mother's still alive; she's ninety-one. She's out in this home at the other side of the city. I haven't seen her now since Christmas – that's seven months – cos I've no way of getting over to her. I'm house confined, you might say, with this ould thing. She's better than I am meself and that's makes me feel twice as old as her. She said to me daughter that last day she went to visit her, 'Is your mother flying her kite?' God love her. She'll see me down; she'll see us all down. I bought her a straw hat and sent it out to her the other week and it blew off her at a garden party she was at. Me daughter had got me one for sittin' in the sun when I went on the MS holiday. So I sent it out to her yesterday and she was thrilled with it. I'd never wear it again, I needn't tell you. No matter where me daughter goes, she has to come home to me and get the dinner and wash up the delph and all after it. After all, she's only twenty-one and it's a bit young to be a 'mammy', as she says.

Most of those with spinal cord injury had already moved out of their parents' home before their accidents and they were also living away from them – most often with marriage partners – five or more years later. However, six of these said that there had been a crucial interlude in their lives after their accidents when they had moved back to live with their parents. Each said that their parents had been very supportive to them throughout the rehabilitation process but that they had a tendency towards being over-protective. Gerry, for example, spoke of his battles with his father:

> I had to fight like the be-Jasus to get my father off my back – to stop the protection bit. It's crucial that one be allowed to find one's feet and to explore the possibilities. The only way

you'll learn is to take risks. If you sit there and say, 'I'm not going to the theatre or pictures cos what happens if I fall out of me chair or what happens if I shit myself?', you're doomed.

Kevin, who had his accident in the early 1960s, said that he had not come up against any protectiveness on the part of his parents. He saw this as being due to the fact that his father had died while he was in hospital and that he had had to become a father figure to the rest of the family when he eventually came out of hospital:

You see the father died before I came out of hospital. I had six younger brothers and sisters and I was kinda put in charge of them. There was none of this pussy-footing or, 'mind him', or that. I used to be out till three in the morning, just came in and went to bed like you normally would do. There was never any bother that way. There was none of this, 'Don't do this, don't do that,' attitude.

Almost all those with cerebral palsy said that their parents were overly concerned and protective of them. While they could understand their parents' approach, they found it to be rather frustrating and constraining. This was how Peter, who was forty-three and living alone with his retired parents, spoke about this:

Me parents are of the old school, you know. They never tried to teach me how to cook or look after meself. Me Ma thinks she can do it forever. The brothers and sisters used to try and have someone looking after me on the weekends when the parents went away and that sort of thing. I would really prefer if they'd all leave the house so I can organise an orgy for myself – get rid of them for God's sake. It's not so much me brothers and sisters cos they've their own lives. Ah, they pop in and all that but they don't hang around wondering what's happening to me. The brothers and sisters wouldn't dream of saying, 'How are you going to manage it hitching?' You either manage or you don't manage. The folks used to worry more. 'How will you get the train?' You know, I'd go to a party and the Da would say, 'How are you going to get home?' I'd say, 'I'm not interested until I have to go home.' I'm not one of these people who goes looking for a lift before he goes to a party. There's always somebody going somewhere so the worries are unnecessary. It takes them time to grow out of it.

There was more variation and flux in the living arrangements of those with spinal injury than those with either cerebral palsy or multiple sclerosis. Six of the ten were living with their marriage partners and in some cases children. Both Al and Paddy were finding this situation most unsatisfactory because of the marital problems which they were experiencing. Al, for example, said:

> I myself at the moment am having marriage problems; not having problems – it's finished. My wife and I are getting a separation. It's getting to the stage now where I find if I hadn't been disabled how different things would be. I'm not saying we wouldn't be getting a separation but I wouldn't be in the predicament I'm in now. I'm actually almost being told to get out of me own house. I'm sitting there taking it all cos again I don't want my son to see myself and my wife arguing. And it's my son all the time that I keep thinking about. Then, being disabled, not being able to get up and walk out of that room makes it all so much harder.

A further three people with spinal injury were living with their parents and siblings. Conor was one of these and he explained how his compensation award had enabled him to buy a house close to his parents:

> I've a sister living here with me. My parents are just round the corner. Me mother is more or less here all the time. At first, the parents were back and forward from their place for meals and that but as time went on we operate the two houses out of the one really. It's a great help.

Finally, there was Dolores who was living alone in a flat. She was separated from her husband and was very proud of the fact that she was able to manage on her own:

> I have one room and a tiny little kitchen, bathroom and toilet. That's it. There's no separate bedroom. It's all right for one but not for more than one person. It's not suitable for a wheelchair. But I'm so used to it, I'm able to manage it. People often say to me, 'Jesus, how do you manage?' but you always find a way. I do anyway.

'We were living in an upstairs flat and it was really impossible'

Houses in Ireland have traditionally been built with the notion of able-bodied occupiers in mind. What happens, then, when disability enters people's lives? To what extent are their housing needs met?

Almost all twenty-six people who were living in the community said that they had had to make changes in their housing situation in view of their disabilities. The most drastic step was moving house while others made alterations to their

159

existing homes. Those who went through these experiences often had a good deal to say about them and saw them as involving far more than just bricks and mortar or even money.

Seven people said that they had moved house specifically because of their disability and the unsuitability of the houses in which they had been living. All these felt that they had certainly gained in terms of physical access but some stressed that the moves had had very negative social consequences. Hugh, who was disabled due to a spinal cord injury and who was living in a local authority house, was one of these. He pointed out that both he and his wife had found it very hard to have to move away from their supportive neighbours and convenient amenities just at the time when they were trying to come to terms with his disability:

> We were living in an upstairs flat and it was really impossible. When I got out of hospital for the weekend I'd really just be stuck in the flat because it was too much to be getting people to carry me up and down. We got a bit of pressure put on the Corporation and got the house. It was a new house – they were only just being built. Again, I'm not that badly disabled and I can get up and down steps and that. But we got a ramp put in for handiness. We got that done ourselves. Through the Health Board, I got a stair lift. I've got a chair upstairs. The rooms are all accessible.
>
> We really missed our old neighbours. They were really great neighbours and pulled in with us when I had me accident. The shopping centre is a mile from here. We had no car when we moved up and there were no buses either so you can imagine the hassle that caused compared to where we were. But we just had no option but to move. It was very rough for those first few years.

Helen, who had multiple sclerosis, said that she had been very reluctant to move away from her neighbours but that she liked even less the prospect of being in an extension away from the centre of activity in the house:

> There were steps up to the front and around the garden at the back. So, it was a thing that we just had to move because we were going to get an extension on at the back and it meant I would have been out at the back of the house. It was a terraced house. I'm glad now that we made the move although we had lovely neighbours and all that. The extension at that time, it was costing an awful lot and I'd have been right out in the far end of the back garden and I said, 'In no way are you putting me out the back away from everything.' So my husband said there was only one thing and that we'd better start looking for a house somewhere and this one came up and the whole idea was to get one with a garage and this was it.

Twelve people in the study said that they had had to make major alterations to their houses because of their disabilities. The parents of those with cerebral palsy said that they had tended to make these changes when their children became too heavy to be carried with ease around the house. In most of these cases, the parents had organised to have extensions built which included a downstairs bedroom-cum-sittingroom and a bathroom. This was how Paul's mother, for example, described the work which they had done:

> Of course, he can't go upstairs. I've things on the flat now for him and it's years since he was upstairs. I'll have to bring him up sometime to show him what's up there. The house had to be re-done for his convenience. He has his own toilet and all inside, shower and that. The old kitchen is his bedroom and then the front is his sitting-room.

The whole issue of house adaptations was highly emotive for some of those with multiple sclerosis in particular. Carmel, for example, spoke angrily about the extension which her husband had built shortly before he left her to go and live with another woman:

> I have a bathroom downstairs. My husband got this done to his own way. It wasn't done for an invalid and he got the grant and all for it and still it wasn't done for an invalid. I have plenty of room but like there should have been a bedroom built on. My young fella carries me up the stairs at night or if I'm really that bad I might lie on the sofa in the sitting-room. Anyway, me husband got the bathroom done to his own liking. It wasn't done for me at all and then he just upped and left.

In contrast, Deirdre, who was a widow, spoke of how she had been spared the trouble of having to build an extension because of her late husband's handiwork when their children were growing up:

> My bedroom is off the sitting-room. See, my husband built that for the lads when they were growing up. He was the best husband that ever lived. He was great. It's very handy to me now and when he died – he died very suddenly – my son said to me, 'You're not going upstairs, the toilet an' all is downstairs.'

Ger, more than anyone, seemed to see the extension which her husband had built as a symbol of her deteriorating condition. She refused to move into the new downstairs accommodation, which had been ready for four years, because she feared that it would 'bring her down mentally and physically'. Ger's husband, on the other hand, saw the extension in more practical terms and as something which he had achieved:

> The time I got the extension built she said, 'No, I don't want it.' Okay, she can still make it to the top of the stairs but it is there now and it's paid for. But if a time does come and she does move into it, that's that problem solved and we have to tackle the other one now. See, we have the steps front and back; we're on a bit of a height here. I want to put a porch on at the back. She loves all these house plants. It would be ideal to have a porch there for her where she could work on these things herself and give her a run into the garden as well at the front. Thinking ahead all the time. If I get it done now while I'm still working away, we'll manage the financial end. The longer I leave it the harder it is going to become for me to do it because in our job the whole structure is changing. Maybe next year I could be out on early retirement. I have to get in and get this organised within the next twelve months and get the job done and over with. If it comes to a situation where she will have to totally rely on the wheelchair and change to a motorised one, well she is going to need room to manoeuvre.

Most of those who had had alterations made to their homes stressed that it was important that their own particular abilities and disabilities be taken into account. Eddie, who had been disabled in an accident, spoke out strongly on this:

> They had started building the extension here while I was still in hospital. The architect that was looking after it, he was a bit of a gangster. He came out and he was telling me, 'The front of your house, it's all on a height; so what we'll do, we'll take the whole lot out and put a drive in and have an electric lift up to the door. You see you'd wheel up to it, push a button and then you're up on the step.' Meanwhile I was

163

doing physiotherapy and we were going outdoors, up and down ramps, you know all around the hospital two or three times. You were getting a bit of strength and would know what to do if you came to a hill, whether to go slow or fast or make a dash for it or what. I said I didn't like his idea. He said, 'Ah well, if the electricity goes you can always put this rope on and you can always pull yourself up it.'

I was saying it to the Ma and Da actually the next day, 'Jasus, could you imagine me there pulling this thing up like a tribesman in the middle of the jungle or something.' So, I said the next time the architect comes out I want to have a chat with him. So, it took me two hours and I designed the front of that house. I designed it the way I wanted it, the way I thought it would work, you see. I had asked one or two of the occupational therapists out there. They have a fair idea like what a certain person would need, like, as regards the height of the ramp and all this crack. So, I showed me sketch to the architect and he said, 'Ah, yeh, that'll be grand.'

About half those who had major alterations done to their houses said that there were some aspects of the finished work which could have been better. One of the commonest complaints was that the extensions were very cold and hard to heat. Anne, who had multiple sclerosis, was certainly dissatisfied with her shower-room but delighted in the fact that her bedroom in the extension had become a key location for family activity and discussion:

I got the extension two years ago – bathroom, toilet and a bedroom. Oh, Jesus, I'll tell you about the shower. I took three showers in that place and I'm never taking another because each time I took them I nearly got pneumonia. I got a grant from the Corporation for £4,000 and they loaned me £4,000 so I'm paying back that loan at £15 per week. If I hadn't been buying my house they would have done it for nothing but the people they do it for nothing for they just lift it over their house and kind of drop it out the back. My sister-in-law has one and a fellow down the road has one. They fell apart.

The whole family comes into me in the morning. I'm in bed and they get their cups of tea and they are all down in my bedroom. They are all sitting round the bed. That's the truth, on the commode and all they do be sittin'. Of course, you wouldn't know it's a commode; you'd think it was a chair. Everything is discussed and thrashed out down in that room.

Debbie, who had multiple sclerosis, was one of four people who said that they had made only minor adaptations to their houses. She was reluctant to undertake any major work but stressed that even small changes had make a big difference to her life:

I got a man to make a slope so that I can go into the garden in the chair. It was great because I could get out before but I couldn't get in. The stairs are handy and I have a walking frame upstairs. I really couldn't walk without it. I could have the house adapted and have horizontal bars which I would hate and my husband would hate. I use the chair a lot in the kitchen but we have steps. We have lived here for twenty-nine years. It would be an awful job to level it out. Oh, we'll manage. You can see where I chip the wall with the crutch – but you get over these kind of things.

Paddy, who was disabled due to spinal cord injury, was in a rather exceptional situation in relation to his housing situation. He pointed out that he was living in a basement flat which was most unsuitable given his disability and blamed this on his wife with whom he had a very strained relationship:

We were in the flat before I had the accident. It's anything but accessible. I've to go down a flight of stairs to get to it. It's bloody inconvenient and, there again, my wife has to bring the chair up and down. Anytime I wanted to move out but she wouldn't come. We were offered a flat on the ground floor and she wouldn't take it – too draughty or it wasn't this or that. She has the place adapted to herself. The settee is in front of the fire, table is behind it and I'm behind that.

'There's always my needs to be taken into consideration'

We have already seen that about half of the people who were living in the community said that they needed assistance with personal care and that most of the others required help with a whole range of less intimate tasks in and around the house. Who were the main providers? What sorts of issues were raised in relation to the giving and receiving of assistance?

Close family, and especially parents and marriage partners, who were living with the people with disabilities, emerged as being the dominant source of care and assistance for those who were based in the community. Parents were particularly significant in the lives of those with cerebral palsy and a number of the mothers pointed out that they had had little or no outside help since their children were diagnosed. Brian's mother was among these and she said that she was sometimes brought to the end of her tether by the host of demands which faced her:

> I always wanted to look after him. I'd never burden anyone with it, with him, you know. He's a tough customer in his

own way. He goes into tantrums, depressions and that, you
know. He and his father, they don't hit it off very well. I can
cool him down better. I understand him better. He'd do for
me what he wouldn't do for you. Now, in me own way I
manage him. I wouldn't ask anyone to do anything for him
when I can do it meself. He's no bother to me. But then, I
have me mother who's ninety. There's times now I do get all
worked up when they all start together. She sleeps with me
and eats with me. Then his father doesn't be very well with
his arthritis. They're like three babies.

All those who were living with their parents said that
they were very conscious of the fact that their disabilities had
placed great demands upon them. Jane, who had cerebral
palsy, felt that her father, in particular, had found it very
difficult to cope with the fact that she was disabled and had
as a result turned to excessive drinking:

It's always still there to me that I'm different. There's always
my needs to be taken into consideration. My parents can't go
away. They went away for their first weekend, on their own
like, this year after thirty years of looking after me. One of
my friends came and stayed with me. See, I think in a way
when I was growing up I was always made to feel, like
'There's nothing wrong with you, don't talk about it.' I
mean, it was nearly something to be ashamed of. I mean, I
don't think my parents are ashamed of my disability but I
know my father likes to pretend that it's not there. I think he
finds it very hard to cope with things and my disability is the
hardest thing he finds to cope with.

I'm not the best at coping with it but I wouldn't say he
can at all. He never talks about it when he's sober but when
he's been drinking he does. Like accusing me really. He gets
really aggressive when he's drinking and it's nearly always
taken out on me: 'Ah you're so spoilt.' You know, that their

whole lives revolve around me and that I do nothing in return. That's been going on now for the last ten or eleven years. When he's not drinking he's the greatest crack and like we get on great but when he is, he's all dopey and stupid and that's what I hate now. That's the one thing I dread, when Mum goes out and I'm left on my own with him.

Danny, who had been disabled in an accident and who was living with his parents, felt strongly that there is not enough recognition of the impact which the onset of disability has on the various members of a family who are living with it:

> If someone has an accident, it's harder on the family to adapt than it is for the person who has the accident. I'll explain to you why. I'm disabled, crippled all the way down. I can't see that; I'm looking out from the shell. But the family are looking at the shell, do you understand? They get a constant reminder all the time by looking at me and it puts an awful lot of pressure on them. It's much harder on the family than people are given credit for. It's very important to get out of the house. The parents and family are sick of looking at me. You have to give them a rest, you know. If I don't want to go out, I have to go out to give them a break.

Paul's mother echoed many of these points as she looked back over the experience of living with, and caring for him, since he was diagnosed as having cerebral palsy:

> He cried for the first six years, day and night, and he is lucky to be alive because I nearly killed him a few times. Day and night, he keened. It came to the stage where my husband and I nearly had a nervous breakdown. But I thought it was my duty to get on with it. It never struck me that he should go

into a home or anything like that cos in my time and my mother's time we had a hard time and you did what you had to do and you didn't question it. You didn't look for help. You just did it yourself.

The only time it happened that he was ever away was when he was about nine or ten and I was sick and needed a break. I asked the doctor at the clinic was there anywhere I could send him to be minded for a week and they took him out to the clinic in Bray. But it was a waste of time because my husband and I walked up and down the beach crying and we went out to see him everyday. And he bawled when he saw us. So, it was a waste of time. The house revolves around them. It's hell with them and hell without them. Do you understand? You're doing so much for them. They do demand an awful lot of attention. He'd be sitting there and I couldn't look his way because I'd get this nod to come and help him with something. So, I have trained myself not to look now, to be honest with you.

Gerry, who was disabled due to a spinal cord injury, was one of those who depended mainly on his wife for assistance with personal care activities and other tasks. He stressed that it is very difficult for a marriage partner having to move between the roles of nurse and lover:

It's very difficult to be a nurse and a lover at the same time and it's very difficult to have to attend to the messy bits. Whereas before, sex might have been spontaneous, 'wham bam, thank you mam' or an orgy or whatever; now you have to worry about the incontinence thing and whether or not you dirty the sheets or you have to have a wash afterwards. In other words, the thing has to be thought about and prepared for. Consequently, all this can result in a phenomenal diminution in sex drives. The husband or wife, whatever the case may be, can be too goddamn tired and brassed off with mopping up after the one with the disability and helping them into bed and out of bed and into the shower and out of the shower and into the car and out of the car.

Similarly, Ger's husband, who had been her main source of assistance since becoming affected by multiple sclerosis, said that he had problems in combining the role of carer and that of worker and family breadwinner:

> Anyone at work who comes along and says, 'How's Ger?', I say, 'Ger's great, powerful, never better.' The reason I say that is because if I say she's not well, they start questioning me and the whole thing starts coming back to you. You want to keep it to yourself, your house and your family. When you are outside doing your day's work, you don't want to know about it, you don't want to talk about it. The biggest joke in this house is when I'm going out I say to Ger, 'I'm going to work for a rest,' which I am. Nobody knows, only the family and the person involved what it's like from the time it starts and right on through the ongoing thing. When she says that she does all these things around the house, it doesn't mean that we won't do them for her. She has to do them. She will actually fight with me. She will turn around and say, 'You're trying to make an invalid out of me.' So I turn around and say, 'Go ahead.' You wouldn't want to be too thin-skinned.

Deirdre and Carmel were the only two people in the study who said that they depended very heavily on their own sons or daughters. Both had multiple sclerosis and Carmel, in particular, felt badly about her situation because she felt that it was inappropriate for her teenaged son to have to attend to her personal care needs:

> Young John, he's a great help. He's like the father in the house since me husband left. He does have to help me when

I have to change myself – down there you know I have these incontinence pads. I thinks it's awful that he has to do that and he only nineteen but it's the only way I can manage. Ah, he's a great lad.

Most of those who were dependent on members of their families said that this could sometimes give rise to serious tension and that they had to be careful not to appear to be too demanding. Anne, who had multiple sclerosis and who needed a good deal of assistance, said that she tried to be patient so that she would not drive the family away from her:

People can get fed up with you very easy. You know, if you say, 'I want this done, do this, do that,' all the time. I'd get very fed up with anyone that was ordering me around. So, if I want anything, I take me time, make sure they're not doing anything else. The whole lot of them, they did rally through it, I'll say that for them. They used to get annoyed but as me husband said, 'After all maybe you're asking them to do too much – think about it. I get fed up with you sometimes so there is no harm in them getting fed up with you.' But then who wouldn't? I'm not just praising meself but there are people that just couldn't get themselves to be so dependent on other people. But the family is great, they really are great.

Eddie, who had been disabled in an accident, stressed that it was a great help to feel that there was some way of repaying family members for their help. He was almost totally independent but said that he felt happy enough about asking his younger sisters to do jobs for him because he was able to give them lifts in his car in exchange:

The two younger ones, they didn't really know what was wrong at the start. Mother and Father told them that I'd be

171

in a wheelchair for a few months but they know now. It doesn't bother them. I do have them running around. If I'm in bed and I forget to bring in a book or the paper or a cup of tea, I let a roar for them. They come running in – slaves, you know. They get their own back. They get their lifts into town so that keeps them going.

Al and Paddy, both of whom had spinal cord injuries, were the only people in the study who said that they were living with family members – in their cases wives – who were not prepared to give them help when they needed it. Both felt very let down by this but said that it had forced them to work really hard at developing their level of independence. As Paddy said:

When I got out of hospital I always needed a hand to get into bed at that stage. I'd ask my wife to assist me and she'd say, 'All right I'll be with you now,' and I'd be waiting and waiting. I think it was that attitude that has made me as independent as I am today. I often remember being stuck in the bath and calling her and asking her to help me out. And she'd say, 'Yeh, I'll be there in a minute.' She'd be watching the television. Bloody bath was freezing, Jesus! There was only one way to do it and that was to try. The wheelchair was beside the bath and once I got up to the bath rim I was safe. That way I'd get up and out into the chair. The next thing the door flew open, 'How did you get out?' 'I found me own way out. Go back to watching television, I'll manage.'

There was always things like that. Anyway, I eventually got to the stage where I didn't need a hand in and out of the bath. I think it kinda disappointed her more – one more thing I could do without her assistance. Maybe I was too demanding at the beginning. I don't know, I don't remember being too demanding. I never wanted to be. I don't think I was ever too demanding. I always tried to be as independent as possible. I always wanted to show her, not just her, anybody, that I could cope with the situation.

Seven people said that relatives living quite close to them had played, or were continuing to play, a major role in providing them with the assistance which they needed. Carmel, who had multiple sclerosis, was one of these, and she explained that her mother and sister formed a crucial part of her support system which also included her son and a home help:

> Now Mammy comes down everyday. She comes down around twelve and gets dinner for the three of us and then she goes up at about half three and gets her own dinner. She still has two boys left at home. Mammy is like another sister cos we do have our ups and downs; we do squabble now and again over different things. We always make up in the end anyway before she goes home. She's sixty-five. She always has a little bit of gossip to tell me. She never comes down unless she knows someone is dead, someone that had my disease and died. 'Mammy, I could live to be ninety cos it's not a killer as such.' Once she hears MS, she's all ears. I do say, 'Mammy, I'm left your road twenty odd years.' Me sister is very good to me too. She comes down every Saturday and cooks the dinner and she cooks the bit of meat for Sunday and peels the potatoes. I don't know how I'd manage without her and Mammy.

Billy's mother recalled how her own sisters and brother had helped out greatly by enabling her to have a break when he was young:

> I had great support. My two sisters and my brother were great for taking Billy when he was relatively young – sort of four or five. The were great and it gave me a break which I badly

needed. They would take him for a day at a time so he mixed
with all his cousins and got out a lot. You see, when Billy was
six I had four of them all young. It was a pretty hectic life
trying to, sort of, do things for Billy.

Dolores, who lived in a flat on her own, said that her
mother, daughter and sisters had been very supportive to her
since her accident and were the main people who assisted
her with household jobs which she found difficult:

Me young one comes in and cleans the place for me. She
hoovers it right down every Saturday. She's started doing a
lot more for me in the last couple of years. And the curtains,
she takes them down but I'd do the washing of them and I'd
let her hang them up. I like to be able to do things myself. I
couldn't reach the curtains; I'd probably go through the
window so she'd do that. My sisters are very good to me and
me mother is the best in the world. Me Ma says, 'Come up
to me and get your dinner.' So, I go up to her every day and
that's a great help.

Friends and neighbours were two other sources of
ongoing voluntary assistance, alongside family and relatives,
for some of the people in the study. Anne and Debbie, both
of whom had multiple sclerosis, were really the only two
people who said that they had friends who helped them with
household tasks on a regular basis. Debbie had a friend who
went shopping for her every week while Anne said that two
of her friends had come and done housework for her every
week for a few years before her husband retired:

I went to Mass every morning before I ever got sick and I'd
meet Mrs Higgins and Mrs Burns. I knew them just to see and
have a chat with but when I got sick, anyway, they came up

one day and said they'd come up to me but they wouldn't come up just to talk to me. They came into me every Wednesday and Mrs Higgins hoovered the house from top to bottom and done all the bits and pieces. I'd be out cleaning the stove with me one hand and Mrs Burns would be pottering around doing her bit cos she's not very able – kind of disabled, you know. They're very good, very, very good to me. They really were. And like they used to get me messages for the day. They're still coming up to me. They don't do anything in the house, just have a chat. They come up on a Wednesday and Mrs Higgins pays me rent for me. I pay her on a Wednesday and she goes up to the rent office for me.

Most people said that they received little or no assistance from neighbours and felt that it was probably best to keep at a certain distance from them. This attitude towards neighbours was well articulated by Eamonn, who had multiple sclerosis:

Well, we know the neighbours and they are very good but the funny thing about neighbours, you try to keep away and close at the same time because you don't want to get too involved.

Helen was one of the few who received ongoing assistance from her neighbours and she was most appreciative of this:

I know all the neighbours to see, they nod into me – the poor woman in the wheelchair – and I nod back. They are very nice and the other side here, they are very good. There's only a mother and son in there and he gets my vegetables every week. He comes into me every Wednesday and he goes to the market for his own mother and he gets mine as well.

They are very nice. I'm really blessed, really and truly, everybody is so kind. This woman next door, she'll always come round or ring and say, 'Look, I'm going to the shops, do you need anything and I'll call in on the way back.' I've given her a key now so that's handy. If I want anything she has said to ring in and you know we're only here three years. I'm very lucky to have her.

Two of the twenty-six people who were living in the community said that they employed private nurses on an ongoing basis to help them with personal care activities. Both were disabled due to spinal cord injuries and had received substantial compensation awards. Conor had just one nurse working for him and was very happy with this arrangement:

I have a nurse looking after me – mornings and evenings. She's here for about an hour in the morning and half an hour in the evening. I started off using an agency and there were a few going backwards and forwards. Then going back a few years, I got somebody permanent. I interviewed a few people. Susan used to work for an agency. If anything happens that she can't come to me, I can lift the phone to the agency and say, 'Do you have a nurse for today?' I find it much better just having the one person cos you get to know them so well and they know you.

Danny was not particularly happy with the nursing arrangements which he had. He employed agency nurses but felt that he would probably be better off with a permanent care assistant:

The nurses get me up in the morning and throw me into bed at night. The only reason I have them is because of the court case and the fact that they could sue me that I got money to look after me and I'm not using it. So, I have to have nurses. But they're not the ideal thing. If I could get a better person I'd get it. But it's not that easy. Getting people to look after you is an awful hard problem. Getting the right person. If I lived on my own it would be a lot different. I've to get someone to blend in with the family, that won't be in the way. If I lived on my own, I could sus out the guy personally and I could live with him. I could train anyone in in a week if they'd say 'yes' to everything, which is hard to do cos you have to do me bowels every second night and me waterworks everyday and they have to look after you.

So, you really need someone very reliable which isn't very easy to get. Other disabled people I know have had all sorts of problems, like being robbed. But, I'm only looking for the part-time person who will blend in with the family, won't be around annoying people. The nurses from the agency are not hand-picked people. If I lived on my own I'd hand-pick someone. I've weighed up the pros and cons of moving out of home and I think I'm better off at home. I don't think my family would like me to move out and I'm happy at home anyhow.

Home helps were another form of paid assistance. Debbie, who had multiple sclerosis, said that she employed a woman privately to help her with the housework. Carmel and Helen were the only two of the twenty-six people, based in the community, who said that they had home helps coming to them through the health board scheme. Both considered these to be invaluable but felt that they really needed them for more hours each week. For example, Helen said:

My home help comes every day, Monday to Friday. The funny thing about it was I had her for three hours everyday when I was on crutches and able to do much more than I am now. But since the recession, and since I've got worse, she's been cut down to two hours. My youngest is on holidays from school at the moment and she's able to help out. She's a great kid. But I'll have to get Jane back for three hours in September because I'm not able to do many things now out in the kitchen. Like, I can peel the potatoes and things like that but to boil a kettle to put on the potatoes is out – too dangerous in the first place.

RESIDENTIAL CARE

Terms like 'residential care' and 'institutional provision' are often bandied about in relation to people with various kinds of disabilities. For most people, these probably conjure up images of large, imposing buildings which they have been in and which cater for unfortunate people who have no alternative but to be there. So, what does residential care mean to people who are on the inside? Why have they come to live in a 'home' and what have they to say about the whole experience?

Four people in the study had experience of residential care and between them they talked at length about it. Each of them felt that they had had little or no alternative but to move into care. For Christine, who had cerebral palsy, the crunch point came when she was diagnosed as having rheumatoid arthritis and felt that her elderly mother would not be able to cope with her increased level of dependence:

I was around thirty when I got the rheumatoid arthritis. The doctor said, 'I don't know what you're going to do but you are going to have to be lifted from the chair to the bed and from the bed to the chair.' He told me that I only had about two years to sort out what I was going to do. So I put me name down for the Cheshire Home and the one problem I had then was how was I going to tell me Mum that I had put me name down for a home. How would that go down?

Anyway, a social worker from the Irish Wheelchair Association told her and her reaction was something I will never forget. She said, 'And all I've done for you and you're leaving me now.' It wasn't that, but I could see her with her heart trouble getting worse and she was getting arthritis and I knew I wouldn't manage in the flat. We wouldn't manage and when I'd fall I couldn't get up. I knew in the house we were in, no way could I get into the kitchen if I was confined to a wheelchair cos the hall was only the width of the wheelchair and no way would I get into the toilet.

Simon, who had multiple sclerosis, said that he had gone from living independently to being in residential care in the space of about two months. He stressed that he had been very reluctant to go into care but that he was even more opposed to his only other option, that of moving in with his sister and brother-in-law:

I went into hospital on a stick and came out in a walking aid. The hospital said that the only place they were releasing me to was me sister's house, a Cheshire Home, a private nursing home or whatever, but not to a flat or digs. Me sister offered to build on an extension to the house they were living in. I said, 'No way.' I didn't want to involve anybody. If she had built on an extension, I knew it would lead to rows between her and her husband eventually. I didn't want to involve anyone in me situation. Anyway, I fought it out with the hospital and I said, 'Okay, if you're not releasing me, I'll stay here.' So, I stayed in the hospital for a month and at the end of the month I was so fed up I said, 'Okay, I'll go to a home.'

In Aisling's case, it was the ongoing drudge associated with caring for her, coupled with the coming of a vacancy in a Cheshire Home which decided the issue that she should move into care. As her mother explained:

> She left school when she was eighteen and then she stayed at home until she was twenty-one. When the vacancy came in the home I said, 'Ah, no, we'll keep her at home.' But there was nothing for her. She was just looking out the window. If she went out at night we had to wait until it was over and go and collect her and bring her home and put her to bed. So then she went into the home. She had been no trouble as a child. She couldn't do anything except look pretty, you know. The weight was the whole problem, the lifting and the toileting.

Paula first went into residential care shortly after her mother, and main carer, had died. She was the only one of the four who were in residential care who was not in a Cheshire Home and she was also alone in having had experience of more than one residential care setting. During her rather chequered career she had lived in five different residential care centres. Her stays in these had been interspersed with periods of living with her sister and most recently of living on her own in the community. She was very angry that she had not been given more assistance to enable her to continue living in the community and was frustrated, bored and fearful of becoming institutionalised in the nursing home where she was now living:

> I was in the flat on my own for nearly three years. I had a nurse coming in every morning and a home help coming to

give me a mid-day meal. I had to supply a person myself to put me to bed and onto the toilet in the evening. I just couldn't afford it out of the social welfare I was getting and you just have to have people you can rely on to come. I want to know the reason why the Health Board won't pay for disabled people who are willing to live on their own and be independent and who want to be independent. I want to know why they want to put them into institutions and why they won't pay that extra little bit of money rather than pay into an institution.

In the home here, there is the one routine – up in the morning, toilet, listen to the radio, watch television in the afternoon, have evening meal and slowly but surely one after the other we are put to bed. You might be the first and you might be the last. There are really only two here that you can talk to and they are not really with it. I'm the youngest; the rest are in their seventies. It would be very, very easy for me to get dug down and say, 'Well, here goes, I'm finished.' You know, sort of lie down and let life walk over me and just say, 'I'm not going to bother, I'll just sit here and watch television, just become a plant.' It would be really and truly easy if you hadn't got the determination to fight it.

I'm putting up with the home at the moment but there will come a time when the bubble will burst and there will be an explosion and then there will be tears on my side because I will just literally get someone to wheel me out and go back to the Health Board and tell the doctor there to keep his home and that I'd rather be living on the streets than go on like this.

None of those who were living in Cheshire Homes came across as being as unhappy and frustrated as Paula. However, they all stressed that they would have preferred to have been able to remain living at home in the community. For example, Christine said:

No matter what way you look at it, it's not my home. It's institutional; you're always under a rule. I wouldn't be in a Cheshire Home if I could manage to do all these things like cooking and getting in and out of bed. I didn't come here for the fun of it; I came here because I had to. I knew that eventually I wouldn't manage. A couple of years ago I looked into the possibility of moving out into a flat or something and having someone come in and help me with the things I couldn't do. But the money just isn't there for disabled people to do things like that. So, I'll just have to stay put.

Aisling said that she saw little hope of ever moving out of the Cheshire Home, but Simon still seemed to feel that this was a possibility, if only for a relatively short time:

The place itself is okay. I can come and go as I please. What I don't like is being stuck here. Like I did an awful lot of travelling. I just don't like the idea of being pegged down to one spot. I won't say this place is ideal. It has its faults same as anywhere else that's catering for a lot of people. Like, you can't please everyone food-wise. I can find plenty to grumble about but you have to take the whole lot into perspective. They call this a Cheshire *Home* but to me it's an institution.

You, sort of, lose confidence being in a place like this and you don't have the same sort of privacy that you'd have at home. I thought about moving out of here a good while ago. What I was going to do was get a job; just find out if I was capable of holding down a job. If I was capable of that I could easily get a flat. Unfortunately, I got a relapse. The terms I would think of now would be to spend three months out of here and go to England and just keep moving. I know I'm capable of doing it.

THE FUTURE

We have just seen that the four who were in residential care settings felt that they had had little alternative but to take up this option and that they saw virtually no hope of moving back into the community. One major question remains, then, in this discussion: To what extent were those who were living in the community concerned about their futures? Did they feel that they would end up in residential care? Or did they feel that they would have other acceptable options open to them as they grew older?

Seventeen of the twenty-six who were living in the community expressed little or no concern about how their residential and care needs would be met in the future. Danny was the only person disabled due to spinal cord injury who gave any indication that he saw entry to residential care as being even a possible eventuality. However, he saw this as being a most unlikely outcome in his case because he felt that his compensation award would enable him to employ care assistants for the rest of his life. He was very relieved that he would probably be able to remain out of residential care in this country:

> The kind of residential care in Ireland at the moment – if I had to go into it – would ruin my lifestyle. Someone will listen if you fight hard enough. I wouldn't go into a home in the middle of nowhere, that's four miles from the nearest pub and up a mile long drive. I'll tell you what I'd do. If I was a young disabled person with no money I'd get onto one of these American scholarships and go over to one of the universities in California and live independent living. I have no choice that I'm disabled but you have a choice, to an extent, about where you live. You can say, 'I'm not going

there, that's it. You're not putting me there. Put me somewhere else.'

Anne was one of those with multiple sclerosis who showed no concern about the future. In fact, she talked excitedly about the family's plans to move out of Dublin to go and live in a rural area, near the sea:

> We always said we'd like to live in the country before I ever got sick. So, we've bought a cottage and we'll be moving shortly. I'm delighted anyway. It was just a labourer's cottage but they put on an extension. I love the country – always did. Even when we were courting we'd have the bikes and we'd go out to Enniskerry or out to the sea. And there's three quarters of an acre and me husband's a good gardener. I'll have me husband, sister, son and daughter there with me. Please God, it'll work out all right. It's for my benefit, that's why they're doing it. I suppose, it'll be a big change but then, when you're sick like this, I mean you're not getting out, are you? It makes no difference where you live. I don't mean not getting out but, you know. I don't think it will make much difference in the country cos I mean I was never wild. I can't do much now only come out in the chair and sit in the room and I mean me sister will be there all day with me and Jimmy will be there himself.

The group of nine who were very concerned about their futures consisted of all seven people with cerebral palsy who were living in the community and two who had multiple sclerosis. The big worry for all these was how they would manage if anything should happen to disrupt what they felt were their very vulnerable care arrangements. All seven with cerebral palsy were living with their parents and they were very conscious that they were ageing and becoming less well able to provide them with the assistance they needed. Although each of these had at least one brother or sister, none considered it likely that their siblings would eventually take over the caring role when their parents were no longer able. Both Peter and Jane said that their married sisters had signalled their willingness to take on this role but that they had firmly refused to consider the possibility of allowing them to do so. Jane explained:

> Actually, my father wasn't well recently and my sister started saying, 'Listen, don't worry, you'll have a home with us always.' And I said, 'No, no, I'm sorry, I won't.' God, it got a bit embarrassing. She said, 'You're certainly not going into one of these "homes".' To tell the truth, I couldn't have lived with her before she got married. You know, she's super to me but I just wouldn't and I said, 'I'm afraid I'm going to have to. Like, what else is going to happen?' 'Oh, we'll build on,' and I said, 'I won't live with you if you build on.' Like it was all friendly, half joking but she was trying to get the message across and I said, 'No way.' So I don't know what will happen but I was telling her like that, I mean, I'd go to her for Christmas and Easter if she begged but I certainly wouldn't be living with her.

There seemed to be a consensus among the parents of these people with cerebral palsy that it was unlikely that they would eventually live with and/or be cared for by their siblings. Indeed, Paul's mother stressed that she was very anxious to avoid this outcome:

> I tried to take it all on myself. We did the best we could for his sisters. We sent them to school privately and, you know, pushed them away from him. I didn't want them to feel, or even when they'd be mixing now, to feel, 'Oh, he or she

won't have anything to do with me. I have a handicapped brother at home.' I have him trained now that if anything happened in the morning that he's going to be left and that he'll have to sus it out, that he'll have to look after himself. He can get meals-on-wheels, or get on to the Wheelchair Association. 'Because', I said, 'you can't tie your sisters down,' and he knows that and they know that. I have told them, 'Don't think that because he is handicapped that your life is to be changed now.' He has his home and there's plenty of help and upstairs he's all right which means he can work out his own salvation.

So, what did those who were concerned about their futures think they would do if their present arrangements broke down? Jane and Derek were the only two of the nine who expected that they would have to go into residential care. Both said that they dreaded this prospect because they felt it would involve a loss of freedom, privacy and home comforts. Jane, for example, said:

> I mean, I'll have to go into residential care and that'll be the hardest cos I've been so used to living at home and being able to do what I want. I would absolutely dread that day, particularly if I was going to be cut off from the life I have now. I've always had the cushy life.

The other seven who were concerned about their futures were much less certain than Jane and Derek about what was likely to happen. It was very clear, however, that they were most anxious to remain living in the community. The problem which they were all grappling with was how they were going to achieve this. Peter, for example, felt that the ideal solution for him would be if he could find an able-bodied woman who would come and live with him.

However, he saw his poor financial situation as being a difficulty here:

> There seems to be a sort of plot to have me move in with a sister and brother-in-law in the eventuality of the parents kicking off or being unable to look after me. If I moved in with them, they'd have to build some kind of a gaff on the back of their house and ruin their garden and the whole thing would lead to endless rows. I've already got my little pad at the back of this house and I've got used to it. If I could move a woman into my room, that would be the ideal. Money is the only thing that is stopping me.

Paul was also quite adamant that being unemployed and dependent on social welfare was a major barrier in terms of enabling him to have any sense of certainty or security about his future:

> Hopefully, a job will come up. I said, 'Hopefully.' And I've got this set-up here. I'm able to do nearly everything for myself. Cooking is where I fall down. I can cook here in me head but I can't do it. My parents won't be here for my lifetime so I'll have to find some way to live independently within this house.

For Ger, who had multiple sclerosis, it was the prospect of out-living her husband and main carer which filled her with panic about how she would manage in the future:

> I'm terrified that he'll go before me. I was going to let one of the children have this house and I'd live in that room there and I'd have me wheelchair and I'd get to the toilet. See, incontinence is the worst. It's very bad. But now I'm after learning that they'll have to get their own house. I'll get that

wall knocked to the hall so that I can wheel out to the toilet
and I'll live here on me own and I'll get a home help for five
mornings and then on Saturday and Sunday my eldest will
just come and keep an eye to see if everything is all right. If
I wasn't able to live on me own, I would sell this house and
I would have to go into a home. I said this to a few people
and they said, 'You're very morbid.' But you *have* to look
ahead. See, I have a very active mind. It's extremely active
and you see it runs away on me and I do be sitting and
thinking and thinking.

Finally, there was Deirdre who also had multiple
sclerosis and felt very vulnerable because she did not know
how she could cope if her unemployed daughter – and main
carer – managed to find a job:

> If this girl gets a job, which she's writing away for jobs, I
> don't know what I'll do. I think she's browned off at home,
> to tell the truth. I don't know what I'd do only for her. She's
> awful good. I'm just after telling me son I'll have to go into
> a home and he's gone off real upset. I don't want to be a
> burden on anyone. I *would* think of going to live with one of
> the one's that's married only they all have stairs and they
> don't have the kind of money that's needed to put in a
> downstairs bedroom and bathroom.

Summary

This chapter looked at the interrelated and multifaceted
issues of dependence in relation to personal care and housing
arrangements.

One point which emerged quite clearly from the study

was that a person's level of independence in relation to personal care can depend on many factors as well as degree of physical function. Social attitudes and the availability of facilities and technology are crucial among these.

The study group was almost evenly divided between those who said that they were independent in relation to personal care and those who said that they needed assistance with activities like dressing, washing, eating, toileting and getting in and out of bed. The people who said that they were independent made the point, however, that they tended to take longer than normal to complete everyday personal care activities and some of them said that the whole area of toileting still remained highly problematical in their lives.

There was huge variation in the range of abilities among those who said that they were dependent in relation to personal care. Some only needed assistance with a few 'fiddly' tasks like putting on tights or fastening buttons. Others, who could not use their hands, were almost totally dependent.

Twenty-six of the thirty were living in the community and four were in residential care. Only one person was living alone in the community; the others were living with family members.

Almost all those who were living in the community said that they had had to make changes in their housing situations because of their disabilities. Seven had moved house specifically because of their disabilities and twelve had had to make major alterations to their existing homes. The issue of house adaptations was a very emotive one for those with multiple sclerosis in particular as they tended to see the necessity for them as symbolising the deterioration of their condition.

Family members tended to be the main providers of personal care to those who were living in the community.

The strains associated with providing assistance on an ongoing basis were highlighted over and over again especially by those who were dependent on elderly parents, teenage children and partners working outside the home.

The two people who had received substantial compensation following their accidents employed private nurses to assist them with personal care activities. Just two people had home helps coming to them under the health board scheme and one woman employed a home help on a private basis.

All four people who were in residential care said that they had had little or no alternative but to take up this option and that they would have much preferred to have been able to continue living in the community. Three were living in Cheshire Homes and one, who was most unhappy, was in a nursing home which catered mainly for elderly people.

Nine of those who were living in the community at the time of interview expressed great concern about their futures in relation to meeting their residential and personal care needs. Seven of these were disabled due to cerebral palsy and dependent on elderly parents. They dreaded the prospect of losing their parents and stressed that people with significant physical disabilities in Ireland had virtually no alternative but to enter residential care if their families could no longer provide for them.

CHAPTER 8

RELIGION

Ireland is generally recognised as a country with a strong tradition of religious belief and practice. The vast majority of the population have been brought up as members of the Roman Catholic Church and surveys here continue to show some of the highest rates of belief in God and church attendance in Europe. Religion can play a hugely important role in determining how people interpret the meaning of life and the various events which are part of it. The onset of disability is one such event. What, then, do people with physical disabilities in Ireland have to say about the role of religion in their lives? How important is it to them? What sorts of issues do they raise about the relationship between disability and religion?

'Maybe God is punishing me but I don't think I ever done anything wrong on anybody'

Twenty-eight of the thirty people in the study said that they had been brought up in the Roman Catholic tradition and the other two as members of the Church of Ireland. What was the importance of religion to them?

There were seven people who said that their religious beliefs and faith in God were extremely important in their lives. Carmel, who had multiple sclerosis and who was very upset about the break-up of her marriage, was one of these:

> You can have remissions with this disease but I haven't had one for years cos I'm kind of in a relapse all the time but sometime maybe, please God, I'll be able to get up and walk. The only thing I have now is hope, like a lot of other people, I suppose. That's all – hope and faith. I'm a very religious person. I haven't always been. When I didn't have MS, I wasn't very religious at all but I still don't go to Mass. I can't get out to Mass but the girl comes round every Thursday. She gives me holy communion and she does the healing prayer over me and she is lovely to talk to. I could listen to her all night. She should have been a saint, I told her. She's a lovely person; she gives me consolation just listening to her.

Brian, who had cerebral palsy, said that he had strong faith in God and that this gave him the strength to realise his potential:

> From a very early age, I always had the idea that saying my prayers in the morning and at night kept me close to God and I mean going to Mass every morning keeps me from getting frustrated. And another aspect too, I did a lot to date which would have been beyond my capacity a few years ago and I attribute my courage to the faith I possess in my religion.

Prayer, and particularly the rosary, was what Eamonn identified as being significant for him:

I pray a fair bit. I'm not a 'holy Mary' but I get great comfort from it. It's again maybe something to do or something. I might sit back and say a decade of the rosary but you get great comfort from it. It's an inspiration. I don't know what it is but I get great comfort from it. I have great faith in the rosary. Certainly, I always make sure that I say one rosary a day, anyway. I promised that I'd never go to sleep – even if I'm out playing poker and come back at three in the morning – I still say the rosary, you know. A lot of it is probably psychological too; it helps you. It's an uplifting thing.

Paula, who had cerebral palsy, also placed a lot of emphasis on the power of prayer:

Prayer is very important. Well, I don't think I could exist without it because I think, so far, it's only prayer has brought me through. You take a drink, great, you forget your sorrows but when you wake up tomorrow they will be just as real as they were yesterday before you took the drink. But if you really pray over something, really sincerely pray, God will help you. I know that because he has helped me.

Elaine was another person who placed great emphasis on her faith in God. She talked of how she had come to an agreement with God as soon as she was diagnosed as having multiple sclerosis:

When I was told what it was, I went to the church. I spoke with God and I told him, 'Okay, I don't know what I did to deserve it but it must have been some awful damn thing anyway that you're sending it to me. But listen, I'll play it my way if you'll play it yours. You look after me and I'll do what you want me to do then.' That's just how I feel and, do you know something, he has. I still look up at him and say, 'Now look at me today.'

There were nineteen other people who said that they believed in God but for whom religion seemed to play a lesser role than for those we have just discussed. There was quite a range of opinion within this group and Deirdre, who had multiple sclerosis, was among the strongest believers:

I just go to Mass and that, wouldn't call meself religious. Though, I fell yesterday in the room and I know you could laugh but God got me up. That door was shut and this door was shut and don't ask me how I got up. Me bar was too far away from me. Ah, I got up anyway by the bed.

Eoin, who had been disabled in an accident, was another who said he believed in God. He pondered on the possibility that his disability was a form of divine punishment:

A Catholic country. I know I don't go to Church. God is probably punishing me. I believe in God. I don't believe in goin' as a hypocrite, goin' to see what other people are wearin'. I'd rather lie down at night in bed and say a prayer or two. I'm a Christian, you know. I've nothin' against Protestants or all these other religions. I've nothin' against these people. I'm not a practising Catholic, you know what I mean? Maybe God is punishing me but I don't think I ever done anything wrong on anybody. Anything I ever did was good.

The idea that God might have been in some way responsible for his disability was also raised by Danny, who was one of the most incapacitated people in the study:

Am I a religious type of person? Yes and no. Religious in the sense that I believe there is a God and no in the sense that, if he wants me to go to Mass, let him give me the use of me legs back and I'll go.

Some of those who were living at home with their parents said that they attended Mass on a regular basis but that this was more to please their parents than because they felt that they gained anything from it in a spiritual sense. Jane, for example, said:

> Oh, I'm not over-religious. I mean, I go to Mass. I would feel something would happen to me if I didn't and I'd hate to upset my parents over it. But, I mean, I'm not over-religious like. It's not something huge in my life and it certainly wouldn't help me to cope with anything.

Peter was another who was a regular Mass-goer but he said that this was more for social than spiritual reasons:

> Ah, I go to Mass on Sundays. I never made a big deal out of religion. I find religion good, a good social thing to do. It's not the total way for you but it's a good sort of hook, a reference point. Like politics, don't take it too seriously. There's a lot better things you could be doing with your life. I enjoy the people who are in it. I don't avoid priests and nuns. I have a lot of good friends who are priests.

Four of the thirty people in the study said that they did not believe in God or any form of religion. All these stressed that they had given up on religion before they had acquired their disabilities in their late teens or early twenties. For example, Hugh said:

> I've absolutely no religious belief. I don't believe in it; I've no interest in it. When I was younger, I had to go to Mass.

You know, your mother sends you; you have to go. You don't get a choice. And I definitely didn't 'get religion' after the accident. I used to pretend to be asleep when the priest came round with communion. You know, things like that.

Both Gerry and Simon, who were non-believers, pointed out that they envied people who had a strong faith in God and who could derive some comfort from this. For example, Simon said:

I haven't been into religion since I was seventeen and that was before the diagnosis of MS. I just thought a bit about it and 'I wish I did believe and then I could blame someone', but I don't believe so I can blame no one. I'd say it's a relief to be able to blame someone.

'Why don't you take him down to Mount Argus for the relic?'

Many of the people in the study made the point that there seems to be quite an association in the public mind in Ireland between disability and religion or the trappings of religion. In particular, they talked about the idea of people with disabilities being considered as 'children of God' and worthy recipients of relics and pilgrimages to places like Lourdes. What sorts of experiences had they had in relation to these ideas and how did they feel about them?

Those who were disabled due to cerebral palsy were really the only people in the study who said that they had experience of being approached as 'children of God'. Billy and Derek both talked of how their parents had explained their disability to them in religious terms when they were younger. For example, Billy said:

> I'm tepid, lukewarm about religion. I believe in God but I wouldn't say I was the most religious person ever. In Ireland there is this thing of being special if you are disabled; that there must be something special about you if God chose you to be disabled. That's more or less what I was told by my parents when I was young. I believed it until I got into my teens. I think I didn't understand fully. My parents are religious anyway. But, at times, I wonder if they wouldn't have been better if they'd told me that I was disabled because of a lack of oxygen at birth, full stop. But I don't know. It's one of those things. I don't know which is better.

Derek was much more critical than Billy of the practice of explaining disability in religious terms:

> I don't go to Church. I don't believe in Churches. I believe in God. I try to be a Christian. A big question mark after 'try' but I try. I think families have tended to go along the lines that God put Johnny in the wheelchair. Like, you have to remember that anything I say is only my idea. I think religion for the disabled is a lot of bull to the disabled. I'm not talking about religion, I'd better get it right – Church. I used to believe and I used to be taught that there was a reason for me being in a wheelchair. Ma and Da, they just said it to me one day.

Most of those with cerebral palsy said that they had often been approached by people asking them, as 'children of God', to say prayers for them. Generally speaking, they found that it was elderly people who asked them and they all said that it tended to annoy them. For example, Peter said:

I could have made a fortune out of the number of so and so's who asked me to say a prayer for them. If I had only charged a penny, I would have been rich by now, you know. My attitude hardened over the years towards people. Like, the old lady comes along and says, 'Say a prayer for me, son.' I do say, 'Why don't you say your own feckin' prayers.' I felt used. Ah, they're well meaning; they're not vicious or bad people but my kind of people are the sort who would come along and say, 'Ah come on, you old bugger you. You're using the wheelchair to manipulate everyone you know.'

Some also mentioned that they objected to people giving them holy relics to 'cure' them. Kevin, who had been disabled in an accident in the 1960s and who was one of the non-believers in the study, laughed as he recalled one particular incident in which he had been approached by a neighbour:

There was an old woman down the road there and when I came home first she'd come down with a medal from St Joseph or St Patrick or a cure from this or that. One Monday she came over and I was in bad humour and had a hangover and no money and I said, 'The best cure you can get me is go up to the pub and get me a large bottle and bring it back.' She never came over near me since. You get people coming over, cures and relics and what have you. That time you'd take it for a while. That time you were gullible; you'd listen cos, you see, the Mother was there and, 'Don't upset the neighbours when they come in.'

Billy's mother said that she used to get very annoyed when relative strangers thrust themselves on both her and Billy with suggestions about relics and pilgrimages:

Even people that don't know him, they'd rush at him with relics and say, 'Why don't you take him to Knock or Lourdes or wherever?' They didn't even say, 'Did you ever think of ...' or 'Have you been to ...?' Oh dear. 'Why don't you take him down to Mount Argus for the relic?' Billy was always much more patient than me. I suppose from the early years we laughed at these people. I wouldn't just pass it over. I'd say, 'That so and so. Why doesn't she mind her own business?' I'd boil over, explode. Oh, there's still a lot of what we call, 'God help yous' and 'the pat on the head brigade' around, the ones that give you religious relics and not a lot of practical help.

Fifteen of the thirty people in the study had been to Lourdes at least once and they all had a good deal to say about this. Most pointed out that their first visit had been funded either by some charity or by donations from family, neighbours and friends. Nearly all, like Al, said that they felt there was something special about the place:

> I am and I amn't into religion. Let's put it this way: I believe there has to be somebody up there. I mean, I was in Lourdes four or five years ago. The family got some money together to send me. That was an incredible experience. It would make the hairs stand up on your head.

Danny, who was also disabled due to a spinal cord injury, found it difficult to pinpoint why Lourdes was 'special' for him but felt that it had more to do with the goodwill shown there to people with disabilities than to its curing powers:

> I went to Lourdes; once not by choice, the second time by choice. The first time I was sent. The priest came up, a friend of mine, and he said, 'You're going to Lourdes.' So, I said, 'All right,' cos he had it all organised, and then I went again.

There's something special about the place but I don't believe there was ever a cure there. I can't put it into words. You have to go there and feel the sense of being there and you see all the people doing good for disabled people.

Brian, who had cerebral palsy and who defined himself as being very religious, was very critical of what he considered to be the patronising approach taken to people with disabilities in Lourdes:

The practice in Lourdes is: I mean, even if you are an able-bodied disabled person, you gather what I mean, you are not allowed to push your own chair. If you are seen pushing your own chair, there's almost an upheaval; everybody is running to catch you in case you run away and you are like a child that the teacher says, 'You did the wrong thing. Go home and write, "I did wrong", one hundred times.' I mean, that's the level to which they would bring you if you allowed it.

This view was echoed by Hugh, who had been disabled in an accident and who was one of the non-believers in the study. He described how he had really enjoyed displaying his abilities and independence while on a visit to Lourdes in the early 1980s:

Lourdes was the funniest place I ever went. You go to Lourdes and there's just hundreds and hundreds of wheelchairs. I'd say fifty per cent of the people in Lourdes are in wheelchairs. It's all hills but I used to come down the hills on me own. We started and we done it for a laugh then. We seen the reaction of people. Like, everyone was getting pushed along in wheelchairs. I just let go of the chair and down the hill, passing out cars an' all going down the hill. The looks you get. Men ran after me; they thought I was a runaway wheelchair. Mary sat on me lap another day and we went down the hill. You imagine everyone over there is used to wheelchairs. They are but everyone gets pushed around. They're not independent; there's no independence there.

Summary

There is a strong tradition of religious belief and practice in Ireland and over ninety per cent of the population is Roman Catholic. This chapter looked at the role of religion in the lives of the thirty people in the study and at what they had to say about the relationship between disability and religion.

Twenty-eight of the thirty had been brought up in the Roman Catholic tradition and the other two as members of the Church of Ireland. The importance of religion in their lives varied a good deal. Twenty-six people said that they believed in God and seven of these said that their religious beliefs were extremely important in helping them to cope with their disabilities. At the other extreme, four people said that they did not believe in God or any form of religion.

Most people in the study stressed that religion and disability are closely connected within the public mind in Ireland. Those with cerebral palsy were particularly conscious of this and spoke of how they had often been approached as 'children of God' to say prayers for different causes. Many of the people in the study had also had experience of being given holy relics to 'cure' them or unsolicited advice about pilgrimages to places where miracles had reportedly taken place. Generally speaking, these approaches were not welcomed.

Half the people in the study had been to Lourdes at least

once. Most said that their first visit there had been funded either by some charity or by donations from family, neighbours and friends. Nearly all thought that there was something special about Lourdes but some objected strongly to what they felt were the patronising attitudes displayed there towards people with disabilities.

CHAPTER 9

SOCIAL LIFE

'Social life' is an expression which is widely used in Ireland. It is seldom, if ever, defined but refers to people's contact with the outside world, their friendships and leisure time activities. This chapter focuses on what the people with physical disabilities in this study had to say about their social lives. Who were they friendly with? What sorts of hobbies had they? Did they go out much? Were they happy with their overall level of social contact?

'Get back in the race, mate; we're not going to let you die under this'

Much emphasis is laid in Irish society on the importance of friends as a source of social support outside of the immediate family. The test of a true friend is generally regarded as being whether he or she remains loyal even at times of great stress, or as the old saying goes, 'A friend in need is a friend indeed.' Most of the people in the study talked at length about their experiences in relation to friendship and for some this was clearly a very emotive topic.

Twenty-two of the thirty said that they felt that they had at least one close friend other than a member of their family. Almost all these stressed that they derived great support and enjoyment from these relationships and that they were a very important part of their lives. Jane, who was the only person with cerebral palsy in full-time open employment, was among these:

> A friend of mine – a great friend of mine, we grew up together – she made me godmother to her first child last year. I see him now certainly every week or two weeks and that's terrific. I made some very good friends up at the vocational school. Actually, I was out to two of them the other night. I stayed very friendly with about six which isn't bad out of twenty. You know, a lot of them have drifted away. The crowd up at work are great crack. We have a great old time. I have a great social life out of it. We go out a lot. It's great. They brought me away – well they were going anyway – to the West last year for a weekend and then we went to Cork as well.

Eamonn, who had multiple sclerosis, was another who highlighted the key role which friends played in his life:

> The family have given me great support and I have very good friends which is marvellous. The 'phone is great because, if I'm ever depressed or anything, I ring somebody and tell them to call to see me. I remember many years ago, one night I was really low and I rang up a good friend of mine and said, 'Listen, I'm really very low. Will you come to see me.' So, himself and the wife came over. They understand which is marvellous. As I say, it's that support that's very essential.

Gerry also felt fortunate to have friends who were there when he really needed them. He spoke appreciatively of their support, particularly at the time when he was trying to come to terms with the effects of his injuries:

> When I got the knock, my friends decided that they weren't going to let me lie down under it and whenever I got the blues and I got depressed and I got bolshie and so on and so forth, they literally came along and gave me a kick in the ass, 'Get back in the race, mate; we're not going to let you die under this.'

The eight people who felt that they had no close friends outside the family talked quite openly about this and most tended to see it as yet one more consequence of their disabilities. Peter, who had cerebral palsy, said that he had quite a range of casual friends and acquaintances but that he had never developed any close friendships. He attributed this very much to his experience of special schooling and subsequent unemployment:

> I don't have any close friends. Well, the way it was, hospital friends; you make friends like you make friends on a holiday or going on a boat. And you think, 'Ah, we're friends, write soon,' and oddly enough one or two of them did which was more of a surprise than anything else. Then, you'd go to school. If I like to think of anyone as friends, I usually gravitated towards people older than me – the physiotherapist or the teacher. I didn't develop this camaraderie with the pupils. Unlike most social lives, mine doesn't thread into a working life. At forty-four, I no longer have a peer group. My age group is gone. They're working or they're in jail or something and I mix with people who are ten or twenty years older or younger than me.
>
> I was at a huge orgy last weekend. We were meant to go yachting but the boat broke down. I suppose you could call it

'a weekend not yachting'. It was a real hodge podge of people. My father often says, 'Why are you mixing around with these headbangers?' I think this is my trouble. I never sort of got together with enough people or fought with enough people to decide that we were friends. Cool man, okay you'd knock around. They'd move on, anyway. They'd have a job.

Larry, who had multiple sclerosis, said that he had cut himself off from all his friends when his condition had gradually worsened because he was 'fed-up with himself'. He felt it was unlikely that he would ever rebuild these friendships or create new ones especially in view of his poor financial circumstances and said that he relied very heavily now on his wife and family.

Carmel and Deirdre, who also had multiple sclerosis and who were separated and widowed respectively, pointed out that they had not really had any close friends when they were diagnosed as having multiple sclerosis because they were so involved with their husbands and young children. Both felt that they were at quite a disadvantage now in terms of building new friendships and said, like Chris, that their families were their main source of support. This was how Deirdre spoke of her situation:

> The only girl that I was really friendly with is dead. It was last year she died. I didn't see her for years and years but when I was married first she used to come out to me and I'd go to her house and that. Her husband and my husband were great friends. They worked together kinda thing. She was lovely and we used to talk about everything. But then we both had the kids to think about. Since this MS got bad, I don't really get out much. See, transport is an awful problem. Like, it's hard to meet people if you can't get out.

Paddy was quite definite that he had no close friends and said that this was because of his wife who had become very possessive and difficult to live with after his accident:

Haven't got any friends cos she won't make friends. You can go to other people's houses and all the rest – I could – but she's not very popular because she's always putting her foot in things. Yet, I get on like a house on fire and I know that they're afraid to ask me because she'd be down like a light on top of them. If I was let out on me own, I'd always do well, get to know people, different people. But I think to get too familiar, that really bugs her. Like, she'd drill holes in anyone. Like, she'd say, 'The face on that one there!' and her own is not exactly the Mona Lisa's either. She can go wherever she likes on her own, doesn't matter whether I approve or not – not that I have any objection – but I don't see why she should object to me.

Most of those who were disabled due to multiple sclerosis and spinal cord injuries talked about the impact which the onset of disability had had on their existing friendships. About half of these said that at least some of their friends had remained supportive towards them. Kevin was among these and he was quite adamant that his relationship with his pre-injury friends had not been affected by the onset of his disability some twenty-four years earlier:

At that time, the hospital wasn't very keen on letting you out for weekends. There were very strict regimental rules. You got out on a Friday night, say, and you had to be back at all costs by half seven on Sunday. I got out a few times with the boys and rambled in about eleven o'clock. The boys are still around. Still have a few pints with them most nights and a game of darts. They all live around here. They're all married as well. It's like going from teenagers to old fellas – all pot-bellies an' all that.

Debbie, who had multiple sclerosis, was another who said that her friends had remained loyal in spite of her disability:

> I certainly didn't lose any of my old friends since getting MS. If anything, we have got a lot closer. I really don't know how I would have managed without them. You know, you need people you can share things with. I try to help them as much as I can but sometimes I feel that I'm taking all the time and not doing much giving. When I say this to them they tell me not to be so ridiculous so I don't feel too badly about it.

The people who said that they had lost pre-disability friends varied a good deal in their response to this experience. Some, like Al and Dolores, were quite casual about it because they saw it as a consequence of their having moved away – in a geographical sense – from their friends in the immediate aftermath of their accidents. Others, including Simon and Larry, pointed out that they had distanced themselves from their friends when they had first acquired their disabilities. Each of these had subsequently come to regret this move and Simon, in particular, talked a good deal about it:

> I totally discarded all friends and everything when I came into the home here. I just sort of wanted to forget. I was over-conscious that I had MS, that I have a disability. It made me want to forget about friends I used to play football with and all this. I must have been over-conscious but I just wanted to forget all that. One or two of them found out that I was here and they call every now and again but I don't make them feel very welcome. I don't make them feel unwelcome but I don't go out of me way. I'm sorry now that I did adopt that attitude because I would like to have them

as friends. I find it very hard to trust people and not feel a burden on them. That's why I say I'm sorry that I lost contact with my friends cos some of them are people that I do trust and that I would feel at ease mixing with.

There were three people who said that all their friends had let them down when they became disabled. Eoin, who was disabled in a car crash, was one of these and he was clearly very hurt by it:

All me friends drifted. If you're in a wheelchair you're no good to them. Some did come back for a few months and brought me out in their cars for a drink and then after two or three months there's no way I'd see them any more. Amazing, really amazing. I know in my heart and soul that if my best friend ended up in a wheelchair tomorrow and I was walking around that I'd never leave him.

Hugh and his wife, Mary, said that their best friends had really disappointed them after Hugh's accident and they felt that problems with wheelchair access in Dublin's night spots could be at the heart of the matter:

Hugh: Friends that we had and went out with regularly, they just don't even bother contacting us anymore. They only live three and a half miles away and it's very annoying.

Mary: They were very good friends. We went everywhere together before we were married and after we were married. The particular guy was best man at our wedding. We really were very close. I got the 'phone in for that reason, cos all his friends had 'phones. He didn't want to get a 'phone but I said I wanted it for his sake – at least to keep in contact by 'phone. They did for a while, then – even having a 'phone doesn't help.

Hugh: I think it's because I'm in the chair. Possibly one of the things that bothers people when you're in the chair is they ask you to go out and they might like a certain place and then they find that you can't get into that place so they have to change it. Possibly that bothers them. I don't know.

Mary: There's a lot of places you can't go – all these cabaret places and then they all like discos and that.

Another issue which arose in relation to the subject of friendships was whether or not the people in the study had built up close relationships with other people with physical disabilities. Eight of the thirty said that at least some of their closest friends had some form of physical disability. Hugh, who has just been quoted above, was the only person who said that all his closest friends had disabilities. He had met these friends through wheelchair sport and clearly enjoyed their company. However, his wife, Mary, was less enthusiastic about the whole situation:

Hugh: All of us in the group, we're very, very friendly. We are all very close. We're drinking partners, parties in houses. There's two, in particular, that I kinda knock around with. We keep in regular contact with each other. We make fun of being in the chairs. We're inclined to over-react at times like badly disabled – every now and then take fits in the chair, just for the skit of it, you know. Or, if we thought someone was listening, 'John, what time did Matron say we've to be back at?' or 'Jim, did you bring me tablets?' We make fun out of the fact that we're in the chairs.

Mary: It bothers me sometimes, it really does. I do say, 'I'm fed-up going round with a gang of wheelchairs, crips.' I find it difficult going round with wheelchairs. I don't like it at all. I don't mind it the odd time, but to go round with them the whole time, I don't like it. They're not really my friends; they're all kinda his friends. Like I haven't many friends since we had to move after his accident. There's not many people to go out with. It's really changed, for me it's changed since he's been in the chair. Before that we were always going out. Like, now it's only once in a blue moon.

Helen was the only person with multiple sclerosis who said that some of her closest friends had disabilities. She was very friendly with a couple of other people with multiple sclerosis and said that she really preferred socialising with them than with her non-disabled friends:

> Nearly all my friends have MS. I still have my old friends coming to see me as well. Four of us went round together and, like, it wouldn't be fair for to keep on the same level of going out with them because of the bother of the wheelchair – getting it in and out of the car. See, we have to choose our places where we go now. The wheelchair is heavy without my weight added to it and I don't want to tie a normal, healthy person down to having to come out with me but we do make arrangements now and then and say, 'We'll meet you at such a place.' I have a better time with my MS friends. Maybe my old friends are trying to be too nice to me where my MS ones will have a laugh over things.

All eight who said that they had close friends who had disabilities stressed that they were very particular about the people with whom they mixed and that they would not accept just any person with a disability into their circle of friends. Gerry, who had been disabled in an accident, was most emphatic about this:

There are coming through my social scene as friends a number of disabled people but I don't have them here as token crips. I have them here cos I happen to like them as people. A lot of the crips I know are a pain in the ass.

Most of those who did not have disabled people amongst their closest friends pointed out that they much preferred mixing with non-disabled people. Derek, who was disabled due to cerebral palsy, was among these. He stressed, like a number of the others, that he had to battle against the view of his parents, and many in society generally, that he should be mixing with people with disabilities rather than with able-bodied people:

> People seem to think that because you're disabled that you should be going round with disabled. Ma and Da were always like that. But I don't like mixing with other people in wheelchairs, never did. It depresses me. No, I want to mix with just ordinary people. After the people know you for a while, they kinda don't look at the chair any more, when they know you well enough. To give you a good example: I was out with a friend and we stopped to have a cigarette and I said, 'We'd better go, it's getting late.' We had to meet somebody. So, he said 'Right' and walked off and I said, 'Come're, push this,' cos he'd forgotten there was a wheelchair. See, it's up to the person in the wheelchair. You have to build yourself that people don't see the wheelchair and *you* don't see the wheelchair.

Peter, who also had cerebral palsy, was another who said that he preferred mixing with able-bodied people rather than with people who had disabilities. His main reason for this was his sense of being totally out of tune in terms of outlook with the majority of people with disabilities:

I've always preferred mixing with able-bodied people. I can't stand disabled en masse. Most disabled people, because they're not moving around, can't pick up revolutionary ideas. Innovation is unknown to most of them. I expect people to come onto my beam immediately which happens with able-bodied people because they've been around the world – 'I did Europe and all that,' you know. These are the people I react well to but most disabled people are not that way. No matter how young or 'with it' they appear to be, I very, very rarely come across a disabled person of my age or younger who is 'with it' to use a terrible phrase. They haven't caught up. It's like sticking somebody in an eighteenth-century gown.

'I must try and have something fitted in – I either plan for bridge or something'

People in Ireland are more or less expected to have various leisure-time interests. Most job applicants, for example, are asked to list their hobbies and there is widespread acceptance of the idea that 'all work and no play makes Jack a dull boy'. Where do people with physical disabilities fit into this picture? What hobbies and leisure-time interests do they pursue? What impact does the onset of disability have on the way people spend their leisure time?

Most of the hobbies and interests which were mentioned by those in the study fell into three main categories. These were sport, arts and travel. Fifteen of the thirty people said that they were involved in some form of either indoor or outdoor sporting activity. These included: archery, basketball, bingo, bridge, card-playing, chess, darts, javelin, snooker, swimming and table-tennis. The benefits and enjoyment which can be derived from active participation in sport were very much emphasised by people like Al, Gerry and Kevin who had experience of competing at a high level in their chosen fields. Gerry, who had been disabled in an accident, described the value of sport for people with physical disabilities in the following way:

> That's what sport does; it opens your eyes because you find a guy maybe six or seven years older than yourself but you know he has the same level of disability and he can do X, Y and Z and you begin to ask yourself, 'Why can't I do that?' or 'Can I reasonably aspire to that?' If you have a tippet of wit at all, about two or three things happen: One, you get jealous; two, you get informed; and three, you get active. And that's the value of sport; apart from the actual physical sense of well-being, it's an ongoing educational exercise of exposure to alternative options – very, very valuable.

Kevin, who had become heavily involved in archery after his accident, said that participation in sport had helped him greatly in terms of re-building his confidence and meeting new people. He felt that archery was a good sport for people with disabilities as it is one in which they compete with able-bodied people on equal terms:

> I found it very tough when I came out of hospital. It was so hard to have to ask someone else for assistance for a thing you should have been able to do yourself. But then I started up in sports, in archery. When I took it up it was so natural to me, even though I'd never been into sport before. I didn't even play football or watch football on telly when everyone was Man United or Liverpool. The archery was marvellous for getting out and meeting people. The club I'm in it's able-bodied. It's a sport where being in a wheelchair makes no

difference whatsoever. It's a sport where you have to be 100 per cent mentally fit. You should have no ifs, buts or doubts in your mind. Physically, you have to be fairly fit, obviously. You must be so confident in yourself. You're just one of the guys to the able-bodied archers; you're competition.

Al, who had experience of playing table-tennis in an able-bodied league, also stressed the value of sport in relation to integrating people with disabilities and able-bodied people. He recalled one particular match in which he had derived considerable satisfaction from beating an able-bodied opponent who seemed to assume that he would walk away with an easy victory:

> Went up to play a match one night. They were all playing in their shorts. I was sitting there. I had me bat up me jersey. This guy came out, 'Who am I playing?', and the referee called out my name and I went over. He gasped, he nearly died. I started acting the fool in the knock up and then we started and I beat him. He went mad. He couldn't believe he was after being beaten cos I was after acting the fool – knocking the ball on the ground and all that.

It was really only those disabled due to spinal cord injuries who were involved in sport at a competitive level. The people with cerebral palsy and multiple sclerosis tended to take part on a much more casual basis and in a more limited range of sports. Swimming was popular among these and quite a few said that they went to a pool on a regular basis. Paul, who had cerebral palsy, was by far the most active of all those with either this condition or multiple sclerosis. He was keen on cycling and his mother explained that she had introduced him to this when he was about four years old:

I bought him a bike in an auction room for £5 when he was young and it was the last £5 in my purse and I had to walk all the way home with it from Eden Quay. I put him out on a passage on it the next morning and from that day to this he's riding a bike. I thought it might help the legs. I thought like it would get him up on his feet. Oh, him and the bike gets on very, very well. And he's able to get up on it himself. I used to have to lift him up and lift him off it. But, like that, when he goes out on the bike, you're still nervous. I wouldn't look at him on the road and then I'm always terrified the thugs will drag him off it and throw him on the side of the road. They would do it in a minute. The doctor told me to leave him out on it. He said, 'You're not going to hold him any longer; you might as well let him loose.'

Eamonn, who had multiple sclerosis, admitted to being fanatical about sport. He played both bridge and poker on a regular basis and said that his life revolved very much around the many sporting events which he watched on television:

I love football. I played everything. I love sport; I love tennis; I love all games. I'm the completest optimist. I think of Carlow winning six All-Irelands in a row. People say to me, 'You're not an optimist, you're a super-optimist.' I do get depressed occasionally, which is something that just falls on you, you can do nothing about. Being an optimist keeps me going because I'm a dreamer. I dream about being the best at everything. I have won the World Heavy Weight Championship six times or maybe won Wimbledon. Okay, maybe I'm being stupid but it's no harm. I play a good bit of bridge even though sometimes I can't go. I'm mad about bridge, absolutely mad about it. It keeps me going. It's something to do as well and I'm mad about all kinds of sport. It's the only thing I watch on the television. I play poker as well with a great crowd of guys. We play in each other's houses every two weeks or so in the winter.

See, I'm always looking ahead. As I say, I'm very fond of sport. Now yesterday, there was cricket, which I know damn all about, but I enjoy some matches. Next week Wimbledon is starting, that's marvellous. Following week, we have the British Open, marvellous. Then, we have the Carroll's in August. Then, we'll have the odd semi-final of hurling or football. I thought there would be nothing today until I looked up the paper and saw that Ascot is still on and the pre-Wimbledon Ladies is on. So, that's great. I must try and have something fitted in – I either plan for bridge or something.

Six of those who had acquired their disabilities in adulthood said that they had been very active in sport before they became disabled and that they found it very difficult to accept not being able to participate like they used to. Danny, who had been significantly disabled in an accident, was among these:

Before me accident, I used to do hurdling competitively. I'd won a good bit playing squash and I played soccer on a Sunday. I used to be a fitness fanatic. And after me accident there's no sport I can take part in – except archery. With the archery, you put the bow into the side of your chair, you pull the string and let the bow go. There's no challenge in it for me. So, there is no sport I can take part in. So, I have to watch sport. Now that is hard, to see other people enjoying themselves when I'm not able to. It's very, very, very, very hard.

Debbie, who had multiple sclerosis, was another who really missed being able to play games like tennis and hockey:

Oh, I played a lot of tennis and we were just a sporty family. The family would play tennis and golf – ah, golf mad and tennis mad. That's when you feel you can't do things – I can't join in with them. I can just step up the reading and that but not *do* things. I swim a bit now. It's not really swimming, it's just sort of flopping.

Writing, reading, painting, photography, playing the guitar, crocheting, and going to concerts, the theatre and cinema were the main arty hobbies mentioned by the people in the study. Creative writing was popular, particularly among those with cerebral palsy. Three of the four who were interested in it mentioned the influence of Christy Brown, the world-renowned writer who, like them, had attended the special school run by the National Association for Cerebral Palsy. For example, Peter said:

> Oh, they all thought in school that I should write a novel. I fancied the idea too but it's perseverance that I totally lack. You know, absolutely doomed to become Ireland's leading writer since Christy Brown. But Helen Keller and Christy Brown and all these people, they brown me off. They make you feel, 'What am I supposed to be doing?' Why can't I be a slob? Why should I have to be inspired? I'm not productive. I write. I have a deal on with one of the girl friends to deliver up a chapter of a novel every month cos she thinks I'm a lazy sod and I need someone to push me along. I'm only doing it for pig-iron, you know.

Letter-writing was one of Elaine's favourite hobbies. She had multiple sclerosis and said that she worked hard at keeping in touch with her friends around the world:

> Sometimes, I'm just too tired to go out after I do the little bit of work that I do around the house. But I love to sit down and write letters. I have lots of friends in foreign countries and I keep in touch with them. And believe you me, there

are very few letters that go out of this house that I don't mention MS to people away foreign. Well, I feel that they might be able to do something, or even Irish people, where money is concerned. Well, you can't run functions and holidays for people with MS without money, can you?

Four of those with multiple sclerosis said that they really missed being able to read since their eyesight had become affected by the disease. Carmel was among these:

I feel like ninety to be honest with you. I was a great walker and that. It's really a tragic disease. I used to walk into town with the young fella by me side. I don't do a lot now. I just sit here and watch the television. It's the only luxury I have. I can't read really. It must be really big print because I get double vision. I can't read a book. I could look at a magazine but I can't read little love books like I used to. I was always mad about them. They'd take your mind off things.

Larry, whose sight was very poor, pointed out that he had started getting talking books from the National Council for the Blind and that these were at least some compensation.

Five of the thirty people in the study said they really enjoyed travelling abroad. Brian, who had cerebral palsy, stressed that he had derived great satisfaction from travelling alone to the United States:

Before I went to America, I know my mother and father and brother and sisters were worried. They were worried about flying, where I'd stay and everything but I knew I had to go to see could it be done. This is what I call going beyond one's disability. My ambition would be to travel more on my own, to show people that I can do things for myself. I mean we all need help to some degree but rather than rely on able-bodied people more I want to rely on myself more.

Simon, who had travelled extensively before becoming affected by multiple sclerosis, said that he still held out some hope of being able to go abroad on his own again:

> I did an awful lot of travelling. If I put my mind to it, I could do it again, just head off. I'd love to do it – go to Dun Laoghaire, Holyhead, Dover, Le Havre – that kind of thing. I'd love to do it. It would be a challenge, nothing arranged, just do it. It would be even more of a challenge in a wheelchair. There is no reason why I shouldn't. I'm, in a way, using this disease that I can't do things. When I really think about it, this disease is not stopping me. There is nothing stopping me. I reckon I'd be fully capable of going on the continent.

'That's my idea – go out and enjoy yourself if you can'

People differ very much in terms of how much social contact they want and those with physical disabilities are certainly no exception. The crucial question, then, is how satisfied each person is with his or her own particular level of contact with others.

Twenty-one of the thirty people in the study said that they were happy enough with their social lives and the extent to which they were in touch with others. For example, Conor, who had been disabled in a car accident, said:

I've a good social life. I was drinking for a while but I'm a
long time off the drink now. I'd drink the odd shandy. I have
a good time. I go to sports in the Wheelchair Association and
various social nights. I drop into friends in the area that are
handicapped like meself. I've somewhere to go all the time.

Jane, who had cerebral palsy, was another who was quite
satisfied with her social life:

I've a great social life out of work and I use the 'phone a fair
bit. I'm usually out at least two or three nights a week. Like
the last week: it's work during the day. On Wednesday, I
went with a friend from work into town for a meal and then
we met those fellas, I was telling you about, for a drink.
Then, we went back to this girl's flat. On Thursday, I went
out to tea again with a girl I used to work with. Friday, I
went to work and we just went out for a drink after work and
I was home about eight o'clock. On Saturday, I went
shopping with Dad cos Mum wasn't well. My sister and her
husband came over later on Saturday. On Sunday, I got up
late and washed the hair and went up to friends I used to
know in school, who got married. On Monday, I went to
work and went to my sister's for tea, which doesn't happen
very often, which annoys her intensely. And then yesterday,
I didn't do anything.

Most of those who were satisfied with their social lives
stressed that they worked quite hard at building up social
contacts for themselves. For example, Danny, who had been
disabled in a car crash, said:

I'm a very friendly person. I'd blackmail anyone into doing
anything. If I want to go to the pub, I get on to somebody,
see what they're doing and hope that someone will say, 'Yes.'
I don't know how disabled people sit at home all day and

very seldom go out. I try and get out as often as I can. Otherwise I'd crack up. That's my idea; go out and enjoy yourself if you can. After being three months in bed, you'd do anything to enjoy yourself. Enjoy yourself; there's no point sitting at home moping every day.

Eamonn pointed out that he much preferred the winter to the summer because he had far more contact with people then:

In the winter, there's always someone calling. It's like a bus station, sometimes. I pity my poor sister having to make tea for them. As I say, it's that support that's very essential. I don't like summer. I find in the winter that I have everything organised, the bridge and the poker and everything and I am always meeting people. But I find in the summer time there aren't as many people coming to the house due to the fact that they have their own things to do. The family might go down to Tramore for the week or whatever and I wouldn't see them. But then the 'phone is great.

Peter, who had cerebral palsy and who was unemployed, was quite the opposite and said that winter had, until recent years, been a particularly bad time for him socially:

Life is very enjoyable when the weather is warm but in the winter it's sheer bloody hell not getting out, not having something to do. I came out of hibernation for the last two winters and joined a creative writing group. So, the last two winters were good. The best part of the classes was drinking in the pub afterwards. Of course, the class was held up three flights of stairs. I used to enjoy having them dragging me up the stairs. I said, 'It serves you bloody right; you shouldn't invite disabled people along to your group if you can't provide for them.' I had a lot of fun giving a lot of people a lot of stick but they were the type of people that could take it.

Most of those who were unhappy with their social lives said that their problems were due, in part at least, to either their poor financial circumstances or to the fact that they did not have transport readily available to them. Eoin, who had been disabled in a car accident and who was unemployed, felt that his limited social life owed a good deal to both these factors:

> I spend me time doin' naught; lookin' at telly, listenin' to a few records or doin' a bit of painting. What else can I do? I've no bleedin' money. I'm supposed to live off me wife's wages. Can't get out any more. I get out once a week for two or three pints. If that's the way the government wants to treat me, I can't do anything about it. I just feel very bitter about it. I've got this bus pass which I can't use which is ridiculous. I could probably get a train. Where would I go on a bleedin' train with an empty pocket? People in wheelchairs do need cars, definitely need cars. I hate even being seen in the feckin' disabled van or bus. That's not me; it's not my style. If I was in a Wheelchair van or bus and I was gettin' a lift somewhere and I saw someone I knew I'd feckin' turn me face. I wouldn't let them see me in that bleedin' bus, even if they know I'm in a wheelchair.

Deirdre, who had multiple sclerosis, was another who said that lack of money and transport were at the heart of her problems:

> I just say, if I had the money I'd get an ould car and be driven here, there and everywhere. See, I'm really what you'd call a homebird, house confined. Now, the last week: well, last Saturday I only came home from the MS holiday which, as I say, was great. I went to Mass on Saturday night. My daughter's husband's sister brings me to Mass. The chapel is just here beside us. On Sunday evening she came here and

brought us all up to her house. We were all kinda baby-sitting. Up to that, I was just sittin' around the place and walkin' up and down.

On Monday, my daughter came up to see me and me other daughter that's here. I was sittin' in the sun with them outside the door there. Monday evening, watched Coronation Street and walked up and down, the usual, 'til bedtime. Tuesday, the same. I didn't go to the day centre cos I wasn't in the humour and I had the runs. I do have to watch everything I eat cos I'm afraid I'll get the runs and I won't be able to run. Wednesday was the same, just sittin' around. It'd be grand if I could get a bus here, there and everywhere. Thursday was the same, the very same. All my days are the very same except Tuesday now that I go to the centre but I'm not very keen on that, as I told you. Then today, you came and it's nice to have a new person here to talk to.

Finally, there was Derek, who was one of the most disabled people with cerebral palsy. He stressed that his social life had deteriorated very considerably in the past few years, and especially since he had been forced to give up his fund-raising work because he was being robbed on a fairly regular basis. He felt that a battery-operated wheelchair would make a huge difference to his life as it would make him more independent:

> I used to have a great life when I was working. But, all my friends, they've either gone off and gotten married or they just have maybe got a job. In the few years, their lives have changed so much that I don't see them. You have to realise that people have to live their own lives. I went away from them at one stage because I was going out with a girl and we were out nearly every night so I didn't see them for three years. Well, once a year we always used to meet and that was Christmas Eve, wherever we were. That stopped when they

had children. Now, my brother comes down twice a week and we go for a drink. That's the only place I go apart from just recently I've started going down to the pub with a fella across the road on a Tuesday, for an hour or so.

Ideally, I'm supposed to be getting an electric wheelchair soon and, if it comes off, hopefully, I'll be able to go into town and meet new friends which I do pretty easily. You see, my life has really changed in the last year; where I was always out, I'm out now only very, very seldom. An odd time, I feel sorry that I'm in a wheelchair, which I never did before. The only time that I really ever noticed that I was in a wheelchair would be if I was going down the street and another wheelchair was coming towards me.

Summary

This chapter was concerned with the social lives of the people in the study. It looked at their experiences in relation to friendship, their hobbies and level of social contact.

Twenty-two of the thirty said that they felt that they had at least one close friend other than a member of their family. Almost all said that these friendships were very important in their lives and that they derived great support and enjoyment from them. All eight who felt they had no close friends tended to see this as an indirect consequence of their disabilities and the set of circumstances in which they found themselves.

About half those who had acquired their disabilities in adulthood said that they had lost all their pre-disability friends. This occurred in some cases because either they or their friends had moved away to different parts of the country, or indeed the world, after the onset of disability. In others, it arose because the people with disabilities had distanced themselves from their previous friends after they had become disabled. In yet others, it was because the previous friends had made it clear that they wanted little or no contact after the onset of disability. Those who lost friends in this way said that they felt very hurt and abandoned by people whom they had thought they could trust.

Eight of the thirty people in the study said that at least some of their closest friends were people with disabilities. The other twenty-two said that they preferred mixing with people who were able-bodied.

The hobbies and interests which were pursued by those in the study fell into three main categories: sport, the arts and travel. A number of those with spinal cord injuries had become heavily involved in competitive sport since their accidents and stressed that they derived many benefits from it in terms of both their physical and mental well-being.

Twenty-two of the thirty said that they were happy enough with their social lives. Eight, on the other hand, said that they had very little worthwhile contact with the outside world. They identified their poor financial circumstances and limited access to transport as being particular problems in relation to developing this aspect of their lives.

CHAPTER 10

WHAT CAN WE DO?

Voluntary organisations 'for' and 'of' people with
physical disabilities have been springing up in Ireland
since the early 1960s. Some of these, like the Irish
Wheelchair Association, cater for people with a whole range
of disabling conditions. Others, like MS Ireland, are aimed at
people with a specific disease or condition. This chapter opens
by looking at the nature and extent of the involvement of the
various people in the study in organisations like these. The
focus then moves to broader questions about how people with
physical disabilities see their overall position in society.

'We committed the unmentionable sin of actually bringing the disabled onto the streets'

Many voluntary organisations concerned with physical
disability have a high public profile in Ireland. For most, like
the Irish Wheelchair Association (IWA) and MS Ireland, this
is probably because of the intensive fund-raising campaigns
which they have conducted around the country over the

years. But how do these organisations appear to people with physical disabilities? What role, if any, do such organisations play in their lives? Do those who join see themselves as recipients or contributors or both?

Twenty-nine of the thirty people in the study said that they were members of at least one disabled persons organisation. Eamonn, who had multiple sclerosis and who was self-employed, was the single exception. In spite of being 'immobile, quite immobile', he did not use a wheelchair. Consequently, it was not really surprising that he saw organisations like the Irish Wheelchair Association as being quite irrelevant to his situation. He explained his non-involvement in the MS Society very much in terms of what he considered to be his relatively advantaged position compared to many others with multiple sclerosis:

> I often thought about joining it. I just never did. Probably should have joined but the reason I didn't was that, okay, let's say, I'm able to support myself, in a sense. A lot of them probably need support, maybe people living on their own who have to get out. But, I have so many people around me that I have all the support I need, really. I thank God every day that I'm as good as I am. When you see some of the poor MSs in wheelchairs, you know.

Three organisations emerged as being of particular significance to the people in the study. These were the Irish Wheelchair Association, of which twenty-seven were members; MS Ireland, of which eight were members; and the Disabled Person's Action Group, in which three had been involved.

Ten of those who said that they were members of at least one of these organisations pointed out that they had only a very limited level of involvement with them. Jane, who was the only person with cerebral palsy who was in full-time open employment, was among these:

> I mean, I am in the Wheelchair Association. I get all their literature but I've never gone to any of their meetings or anything like that. I've got one friend who is disabled but I never see her, she's just a 'phone friend. It's just that all my friends for say the last ten or twelve years have all been able-bodied and I suppose I feel I have enough, you know what I mean. Probably, if I was bored or looking for something to do, I might, but I've never felt a need for it. I'm not the kind that would be going off to the Irish Wheelchair Association on my own. I'm not that outgoing. I'd need a friend with me and none of my friends would be really ... If I felt I needed it, I'd say I would get more involved but I don't feel at the moment that I do, you know. I feel I have enough in my life without it.

Debbie, who had multiple sclerosis, was another who had very little contact with organisations for people with disabilities. She said that she stayed away from MS Ireland quite deliberately as she did not like mixing with other people with the disease:

> I really don't want to hob-nob with people with MS. I don't belong to the MS Society and go to see what is happening down there. I'm not necessarily going to get like them so why look at them? It might seem silly but I would really hate to compare notes with people with the same disease. Everybody, but everybody is different. The Wheelchair Association in Clontarf is a great place. I go there if there's anything wrong with my wheelchair. I've, sort of, kept up with the fellow out there and I can always go to him if I've any problems with the chair. It's a great place and they are all disabled people working there. It just shows what you can do when you see all these people who are disabled.

229

Ger, who also had multiple sclerosis, explained that she had avoided such organisations over the years because she had suffered from severe depression since developing the disease and did not feel that she could cope with going to any meetings or functions:

> I only wrote to the MS Society recently. They asked me on the form if I want to become involved and, you see, I said, 'No' because I didn't know what that meant. You see, I'm not ready to break away from me family yet. We still go on holidays and I like to go out for a drink with me husband and I don't like going without him. Now, I'm in the local branch of the Wheelchair Association and they wanted me to go out to a cabaret one night but we were short of money at the time and I wouldn't go without him. I'm just not ready yet.

Eddie, who had been injured in an accident, differed from Ger, in that he said that his lack of involvement with organisations, and the Irish Wheelchair Association in particular, stemmed from the fact he felt that he already led a very full and active social life:

> I've no dealings at all really with the Wheelchair Association. I feel that's – how would you say? – you know with blacks and whites in South Africa. I'm not preaching or anything but I feel this is the way the IWA are. Okay, I'll admit there is people that are twisted up and they can't fend for themselves, they can't organise their own social night out or maybe their mind is gone, they can't concentrate long enough on anything. Okay, they're great for people like that. But me personally, I don't have anything to do with them. First, I don't find the time. I think I have a hectic enough life between work, social life, you know, saving to get married. I just wouldn't have time. If you want to go into an

organisation like that and try to help people or even just be in a social club like that, you have to devote some sort of time to it, time or work or energy or whatever. I just wouldn't have the time, you know.

Four people, all with spinal cord injuries, said that their only involvement with organisations was with the sports section of the Irish Wheelchair Association. Kevin, who had been disabled in a car crash in the early 1960s, was among these and he remembered the early years of the Irish Wheelchair Association with a certain amount of nostalgia:

> I gave up the IWA a long time ago. I was involved in it in the beginning. They started it for doing sports – archery, table tennis and that – and we hadn't the money to buy the equipment so we started it to get money to buy the equipment and then the money started flowing in from every direction and we didn't know what to do with it. Next thing, we moved into an office; next thing a chief executive came, this body came and there was no disabled people working in it at all. It was all big stuff. It got beyond our heads. I stayed in it for a few years. It got that if you were a disabled person there, you weren't wanted. It was only able-bodied persons that could run around and all that. I don't know what they do now but they weren't helpin' no one at that time. You'd have to buy all your sports equipment and that's what it was originally set up for.

Al, who had been injured in the mid-1970s, was very enthusiastic about the Irish Wheelchair Association and said that he hoped to be able to pay the organisation back, through helping in sport, for all he had gained from it:

> For anyone who is not a member of the IWA, it's crazy. It's a great atmosphere, a great crowd of people and everybody

backs everybody else. We've got some people in the IWA who are so up on the political end of it. Politically, they are sound. They know what road they are going down and they are pushing their point all the way. I'm not great on politics but I'd like to be more involved with the disabled in so far as being more helpful cos I owe a lot to the likes of the IWA and things like that and I'd like to be able to pay them back. Not saying they'd want me to pay them back but I feel I owe them that much. I reckon it will come to pass cos I told them that, if anyone wants to come down to the IWA and start off in my particular sports, that I'd be the first one to help.

There were eight others who said that their main involvement with organisations consisted of going to social functions organised by them. Each of these said that they generally enjoyed these outings and that they looked forward to them. This was how Elaine, for example, spoke of the social evenings organised by MS Ireland:

Oh, I am involved with the MS. We have lovely evenings out. Oh, God knows there is no-one would stand in front of me and tell me that MS patients are neglected. They are not. We have beautiful socials and they are all very, very sweet. When I see the committee we have, they are really marvellous. They do all the cooking for that social – bake everything. They are really marvellous.

Carmel was another who was a regular attendee at meetings held by MS Ireland. She pointed out, though, that she was much less involved with the Irish Wheelchair Association:

I'm in the MS for years and years. I go to the meetings and all and we get a lovely tea and then maybe have a bit of

music. We do be conversing with one another and asking
how long they've had it and how long you've had it. You do
be judging how bad they are to you or maybe it didn't go any
further with them, thank God. I'm a member of the
Wheelchair but I don't go to their meetings. I went once and
I saw very bad cases in wheelchairs and I was outside the door
and I was crying for two hours and a man came up then and
he said, 'I have MS.' He said he'd had it for thirty years. I was
looking at him and says he, 'Does that cheer you up?' I never
went back to any of their meetings but I'm still a member and
I still get their literature an' all.

Paula, who had cerebral palsy and who was living in a
nursing home against her wishes, said that she enjoyed going
to 'socials' run by the Irish Wheelchair Association. She felt,
however, that the various organisations for people with
disabilities in Ireland were quite limited in what they could
do for people who were in her sort of situation:

> There is no organisation yet has come up to me to say, 'Well,
> come on, we'll help you.' I know the Wheelchair does their
> very best. But in Ireland, unfortunately, there isn't much
> scope for disabled people. There's far more of a scope in
> England and in America and all over the world than there is
> here. I think that's because the country is so small and the
> population is not aware of the means that are needed for
> disabled people.

Eight people said that their experience of these
organisations included being involved at committee level.
They stressed that they were strongly committed to asserting
the rights of people with disabilities in society and that such
organisations could play a key role in challenging dominant
images of disability which they believed were based very

largely on notions of dependence and passivity. Both Christine and Peter, who had cerebral palsy, said that the protest marches, organised by the Disabled Persons' Action Group in the early 1980s, were particularly significant in the sense that they marked a 'coming out' of people with physical disabilities in this country which contrasted very much with their childhood memories of people with disabilities being kept out of public view. This was how Peter put it:

> The DPAG made a lot of noise and it made a lot of very unpopular noise. You can't truthfully say that it instigated action because there were a lot of organisations that were doing much the same thing. However, what we did was real headbanger stuff. We invaded Leinster House. We committed the unmentionable sin of actually bringing the disabled onto the streets – showing off crutches and all the rest of it.

Gerry, who had been injured in a car crash, was the only person with either spinal cord injuries or multiple sclerosis who was involved at a political level in any form of organisation for disabled persons. He explained that he had always tended to side with the underdog and that, in the years after his own accident, he had come to see the disadvantaged position of people with disabilities as a form of social injustice which had to be fought:

> Three weeks before my accident if you'd asked me what a wheelchair was or where was the National Spinal Injuries Unit, I wouldn't have been able to tell you. But, things certainly changed! It struck me like a thunderbolt after the accident that it's a basic civil rights issue. Disability is only peripheral, it's a social injustice. My anger, I hope, is positive. I'm damned if Joe Bloggs coming after me will have to fight

the system in the same way I had to. We haven't the muscle to be in the business of physically changing the world; we have to persuade the world to change to accommodate us. The way to do it is to almost embarrass them into changing, saying, 'Look, now, fair is fair. If you change that, that and that, I can function.'

Most of those who were politically involved in organisations for disabled persons said that they were strongly opposed to militancy as a means of trying to improve the situation of people with disabilities as they felt that it only served to alienate the public and perpetuate the segregation which they were trying to eliminate. For example, Brian argued:

> By being aggressive, you can get the thing done quicker but I don't go along with it because we'd be creating a false image to the public. The public will say, 'Those disabled people, they'll cause a rising.' I mean, if you start creating animosity you'll be put down. I mean, by all means ask the public to join in. By all means. That's what we want but what we don't want is for the public to say, 'Ah you're disabled, you're a farmer, you create havoc whenever you want anything.'

'If it weren't for you, we could go in there'

Everybody stands back from time to time to take stock of his or her life. We look at the way in which the past has shaped the present and hope to learn lessons for the future. How, then, do people with physical disabilities in Ireland see their overall situation in society? Do they feel that there have been many changes over their lifetime? And most importantly, what do they see as being the best way forward as we move towards the end of the twentieth century?

There was a general consensus among those in the study that the lot of people with physical disabilities improved significantly in Ireland over the fifty years or so since the late 1930s. Paula, who was the oldest person with cerebral palsy, having been born in 1938, was most emphatic about this. However, like most of the others, she was quick to add that the existing situation was far from satisfactory:

> Schooling was the worst aspect because they hadn't got the facilities and they didn't understand and if you weren't able to write the ordinary way that every child wrote you were just left behind. Like, for instance, when I'm writing I put my little finger around the side of the table to keep it steady – now they didn't understand that that was the only way I could write. And, like, they hadn't got any tape recorders. If I wanted to do an exam, you couldn't, no matter how intelligent you were – you couldn't write quick enough – and when you hadn't an exam behind you you were no good.
>
> But things have improved now to the degree that they have these facilities for children and for the handicapped but yet I think there is an awful lot to be done. I think socialising with others is the biggest barrier and to try and get every person to understand that we want to be part of the community where we're living. We don't want to be pushed up into a bedroom or into a back room just because we mightn't be able to use our left arms or mightn't be able to walk.

Peter, who was in his forties and also disabled due to cerebral palsy, was another who welcomed the progress which had been made but stressed that many gaps still existed:

I mean in my day it was the business of the sick to be sick and say prayers and, sort of, wait for heaven. Now, there's kids today who go to school in wheelchairs and they're doing a full workload and they're coming home and they've already got a target for the next five years. They may end up in university you know; they may actually get a job. They've got a target now because society has been forced to recognise their validity as earners, producers, whatever you like to call it.

There is a terrible lack of interest shown by the able-bodied in whether or not you're working, have a spouse or kids. The assumption being that he or she is technically still a child. There has always been in my experience a tendency or a non-tendency of the able-bodied to ask what you are working at. They don't expect you to work, they don't expect you to have kids. They don't expect you to have a wife or a hubby or whatever. And this has been one of the most glaring omissions by the able-bodied, whether they like it or not, that they don't expect much from the disabled.

Kevin, who had been injured in a car crash in the early 1960s, echoed these views:

That time, like you know, a wheelchair was completely different. There wasn't so many out on the streets. You might see one every twelve months and that would be a spastic child or something. No matter where you'd go, everybody would be lookin' at you, fallin' all over you and this kind of thing. Then, they started to adapt to wheelchairs. People that had accidents were a different breed back when I had mine. They were more crack. You never knew where you'd end up. But, they seem to be a different breed now – they're more sensible. They seem to be more grown-up for their age than we were. But the main problem is with social life – transport is one, access to places and all that. And we'll say you can get a grant for cars an' all but you have to be workin'. Where do you get a job, like? It's impossible to get a job if you're disabled.

Twenty of the thirty people in the study stressed that many of the most significant difficulties which they encountered in their lives were largely due to the social attitudes which surround disability in Ireland. Most of these identified poor physical access for people using wheelchairs as being the most obvious manifestation of social barriers which exist in practically all spheres of life. Eoin, who had been injured in a car crash, was one who felt very strongly that people with disabilities are victims of discrimination in society. He was unemployed and argued that his lack of success in securing work had far more to do with employers' attitudes than with his actual ability to do a job:

> If I was walkin' around and bleedin' not workin', I'd blame meself. I was never like that. When I was walkin' around, I was always workin'. I was never a day idle in me life. I mean there's no one goin' to teach me how to get a job cos I know how to get a job if they'd take a person in a wheelchair. Knowin' the things I know now, and if I had the money and I had a factory, I'd employ everyone in wheelchairs. Not because I'm in a wheelchair, just to make more money, just to be sensible about it, not bein' greedy. People who are in wheelchairs are the best people to have feckin' workin' for you. They're loyal and they want to work. The wheelchair doesn't bother me, it's what comes with it that bothers me. All the messin' about you get from other people.

Gerry talked in more general terms about the frustration associated with knowing that one's quality of life could be greatly improved if only society were more accommodating to people with disabilities:

I could be described as fairly well balanced – a chip on both shoulders! It's just an ongoing struggle. It's a perpetual pain in the bum, a continual annoyance to realise, as I know for a certainty, that there are many people in this country who suffer from disability who could, if certain societal, environmental and institutional barriers were reduced and/or eliminated, enjoy a far more productive life.

This point was also expressed in a very personalised way by Hugh who spoke of the hurt which he felt when his children blamed him, rather than the planners, for not being able to get into various premises:

> For the kids, there's not many places I can get into. Like, if we come to a place that's really not accessible the kids say, 'If it weren't for you we could go in there.' When we were on holidays last year, there was loads of places I couldn't get into and the kids were real disappointed and they blamed it on me, 'It's all your fault cos you're in a wheelchair.' That bothers me. It hurts.

Simon was the only person with multiple sclerosis who highlighted the social barriers faced by people with physical disabilities. The others tended to see the physical and psychological effects of their disease as being their main 'enemy'. Elaine was typical of these:

> The whole thing for anybody who is diagnosed MS and I have told it to them myself, just say, 'Okay, I have it but I'm going to beat it.' I've tried to do that for myself and with other patients. I talk to them and they'd be sort of crying and I say, 'Don't. Fight, fight, that's the whole thing.' I know you can't get the cure and that kind of thing but at least you can put yourself in front of yourself and say, 'Well, I'll fight it, I

won't let it keep putting me down.' And I think it's a good way. I mean if you did just lie back, lie back down and say, 'Well, I have it now, I'm finished, my life is finished,' well then what's going to happen? What *is* going to happen then? Your life *is* gone and finished.

The importance of effort and determination on the part of people with physical disabilities was highlighted by everybody, irrespective of whether they saw their disabling condition or societal attitudes as being their main adversary. Debbie, who had multiple sclerosis, felt quite strongly about this:

> It's how you approach it. You could sit and do nothing but I would die of boredom, I really would. I mean, if you don't try, there is nobody going to come and help you. You've got to make the effort. You can't sit like a pudding and expect others to do it all for you.

Anne, who also had multiple sclerosis, spoke along very similar lines:

> I was on holidays two years ago and the kids used to pull me along the strand on an air bed. It was better than the chair, wasn't it? Since I got into this chair, I've done things that I wouldn't have dreamed of doing before I got into this thing. No one is going to take pity on you and do it for you so you might as well do it. If you do wild things, people take notice of you. If you're placid, they won't know you're there.

Gerry, who had been injured in a car crash, felt very strongly that people with physical disabilities need to work at persuading society to change rather than just hoping for improvements in their situation:

I talk about 'the struggle'. Now there's no use bemoaning the fact that once you are disabled there is a struggle. The fact is that you are confronted with a set of problems and you have to tackle those problems. If you respond to the situation by screaming 'injustice, discrimination, bang, bang, bang' and doing nothing about it, as a lot of my disabled colleagues do, nothing will ever get changed. The way to get progress is to chip away quietly at the edifice and undermine and use strategies and plans and so forth.

An air of optimism concerning the future for people with physical disabilities in Ireland was discernible within the group as a whole but what was stressed repeatedly was that people with physical disabilities themselves must be central players in the process of change. The delicate complexity of the challenge which lies ahead was depicted by Brian in the following way:

> See, there's two kinds of disabled persons. There's the disabled person who wants to get out in society, who doesn't, and quite rightly too, accept the fact that he can't get into a picture house or a dance hall or that he can't even get married. We fight for our rights. But, there is the disabled person, who once they are told they can't do anything, would appear to accept that teaching. I think, also, that we as disabled people can do a lot ourselves. Society has been made aware of disabled people but there is still a lot of grassroots work to be done, which I have no doubt will be achieved. I think that we are beginning to eliminate a lot of the barriers. But, as I pointed out, we ourselves are going to be the victims of our own downfall if we don't assert ourselves to the life of society.

Summary

This chapter focused on the extent and nature of the involvement of the people in the study in organisations 'for' and 'of' people with disabilities. It also looked at how they perceived the overall position of people with disabilities in Irish society.

Twenty-nine of the thirty people were members of at least one organisation for disabled persons. The three organisations which emerged as being most significant in their lives were the Irish Wheelchair Association, MS Ireland and the Disabled Persons' Action Group. The nature and extent of their involvement in these organisations varied quite considerably. At one extreme, ten said that their involvement had been very limited over the years and restricted to receiving literature and/or attending an occasional meeting or function. At the other extreme, eight said that they had considerable experience of such organisations and had been involved at committee level at some stage.

There was a general consensus among those in the study that the lot of people with physical disabilities in Ireland had improved significantly over their life span, or from the late 1930s to the mid-1980s. However, most stressed the point that the existing situation was far from satisfactory and that people with disabilities were very much handicapped by a whole range of social barriers which prevented them from realising their full potential. On the whole, they were optimistic about the future for people with disabilities in this country but felt strongly that people with disabilities must themselves be involved as full participants in the process of changing the existing situation.

Epilogue

It is now almost ten years since the interviews discussed in this book were carried out. What, if anything, has changed for people with significant physical disabilities in Ireland? Have these changes come soon enough to have a positive impact on the lives of the people who took part in the study? Are the prospects any brighter for younger generations of people with disabilities?

A number of important developments relating to people with physical disabilities have indeed occurred in Ireland within the past decade. These changes have taken place at two broad but interrelated levels which will be discussed in turn below. The first relates to attitudes and awareness of disability and the extent to which the voices of people with physical disabilities are at last being heard. The second relates to actual changes in provision and opportunities for people with physical disabilities across the various spheres of life.

'We have to persuade the world to change to accommodate us'

The decade since the mid-1980s has seen some important milestones in terms of awareness-raising about the requirements and potential of people with significant physical disabilities. A key aspect of many of the developments which have taken place is that they have been led by people who themselves have disabilities. This marks a crucial break from the previous dominance of non-disabled 'professionals' in the disability field, an issue highlighted in the Introduction.

One of the early developments which began to open up awareness and discussion about disability issues was the launching of a radio programme dealing with disability on RTÉ in 1988 called *Not So Different*. The presenter, Donal Toolan, is himself a person with a disability and the content of the programme reflected from the outset a social rights approach as opposed to the medical model of disability.

The link between media exposure and the politicisation of disability became quite evident in the early 1990s when Donal Toolan was the first person with a disability to be appointed to the prestigious Council of State which advises the President – in this case President Mary Robinson. Around this time, Toolan was instrumental in establishing the Forum of People with Disabilities which is very much an organisation 'of' rather than 'for' people with disabilities. Central to the Forum's philosophy is the importance of defining disability as a social rights, rather than a charity or personal tragedy, issue. Although it is still very young, the Forum has gained a degree of political acceptance and influence which could only have been dreamt about by earlier organisations 'of' people with disabilities such as the Disabled Persons' Action Group which was formed in the late 1970s.

Further impetus was given to consciousness-raising about disability in 1992 when a television series, *In From the Margins,* was presented on RTÉ television at prime time viewing hours. Donal Toolan was again involved and the combination of his media and political activities have proved to be important rallying points for many people with significant physical disabilities in this country.

History was also made in 1993 when Brian Crowley, who is a wheelchair-user, was appointed to the Irish Senate. He was later elected to the European Parliament and his involvement in national and international politics was given a good deal of media coverage. This emphasised both the potential of people with disabilities and the barriers which they can face in public life.

The setting up of two Disability Equality Trainer Networks under EU Horizon Programme Funding in 1992-96 were other significant stepping stones in terms of raising awareness of disability in which people with disabilities themselves are to the fore. These programmes involve training people with disabilities on equality issues and they subsequently provide training on these matters to employers and local groups in both the statutory and voluntary sectors.

At an international level, one of the most important developments of the past decade in terms of consciousness-raising about disability issues was the adoption by all member states of the United Nations, including Ireland, of the *Standard Rules on the Equalisation of Opportunities for Persons with Disabilities* in 1993. The *Standard Rules* relate to all areas of social and economic life and while they are not compulsory, they imply a strong moral and political commitment on the part of states to take action for the equalisation of opportunities for people with disabilities. A monitoring mechanism has been put in place by the United Nations to further the effective implementation of the *Standard Rules* in the various member states.

Another significant international influence which has had a major impact on the Irish situation has been the spread of the Independent Living Movement to this country within the past five or six years. The Independent Living Movement, which began in the United States in the early 1970s, is based on the philosophy that people with disabilities should have control of their own lives and the right to live in an environment which is free from social and environmental barriers. Those associated with the Independent Living Movement in this country have been very vocal on a wide range of issues and have been instrumental in raising awareness particularly around the key role which can be played by personal assistants and accessible transport in the lives of people with significant physical disabilities.

There have been two key developments in the Irish context since 1993 which suggest that the disability issues have now been placed firmly on the social and political agenda of this country and that people with disabilities are now being formally recognised as having a major role to play in formulating policy in this area. The first of these was the establishment of a Commission on the Status of People with Disabilities by the Minister for Equality and Law Reform in 1993. The Commission is due to report in 1996 and its terms of reference include the following which indicate a social rights perspective:

- To advise the Government on the practical measures necessary to ensure that people with a disability can exercise their rights to participate to the fullest extent of their potential in economic, social and cultural life.

- To make recommendations setting out necessary changes in legislation, policies, practices and structures to ensure that the needs of people with disabilities are met in a cohesive, comprehensive and cost effective way.

People with disabilities, their educators, carers or family make up 60 per cent of the membership of the Commission with the other members coming from voluntary and statutory organisations and other interested groups. The Commission has made strenuous efforts to seek out the views of people with disabilities, regarding their circumstances and the changes which they feel are necessary. In particular, it invited submissions from people with disabilities and other interested parties, and organised Listening Meetings at a large number of venues throughout the country. These consultations were undoubtedly the most far-reaching and direct in relation to people with disabilities, in the history of the state.

The second notable development of the very recent past has been the progress which has been made towards the setting up of a Council for the Status of People with Disabilities in line with a commitment made by the Minister for Equality and Law Reform. It is envisaged that the Council will provide a representative structure for people with disabilities, through which they can have access to decision-making matters of concern to them. An Ad-Hoc Establishment Group has been given responsibility to put in place a Provisional Council, following detailed consultation with people with disabilities and other interested parties. The Council will be structured from the bottom-up and will operate at county, regional and national levels. The majority of those on the Council will be people with disabilities. Parents, partners, relatives, advocates and organisations 'of' people with disabilities will also be represented.

To conclude, it is interesting to note that Awareness-Raising was identified within the United Nations' *Standard Rules* as the first precondition for equal participation of people with disabilities. Given the various developments which have been outlined in this section, it is clear that major steps have indeed been taken in Ireland in this regard within the past decade. What is particularly significant is the extent to which people with disabilities are themselves becoming more and more involved in the whole policy-making process.

'Look now, fair is fair. If you change that, that and that I can function'

This section focuses on the question of whether or not there have been significant changes in terms of actual provision and widening of opportunities for people with physical disabilities in Ireland in the decade since the mid-1980s. The answer to this must be a qualified 'yes' and a number of the most important developments will be outlined below. However, it must also be recognised that these changes only represent potential beginnings of a new era in this country and that they still remain too patchy to allow people with significant physical disabilities to realise their full potential across the various spheres of life.

Improving communication about the diagnosis and prognosis of a disabling condition

It was clear from the experiences of the people in the study that greater sensitivity was needed in relation to the way in which people with disabilities were initially told about the nature of their conditions and their prognoses. A number of initiatives relevant to this area have been put in place within the past decade and they should go at least some way towards improving the very early experiences of people who have just become disabled. One of these was the emergence of *A Charter of Rights for Hospital Patients* in 1991 which has raised awareness about the rights and requirements of patients.

Another important development has been the growing emphasis on improving the communication-skills of hospital personnel. However, it must be said that a good deal still remains to be done in terms of fully incorporating communication-skills training into the courses followed by medical and para-medical students.

At a more specific level, it should also be noted that the National Multiple Sclerosis Care Centre, which was established in Dublin in 1987, provides special niche periods for people who are newly diagnosed so that they can be given every assistance to come to terms with their new situation and learn about possible approaches to dealing with it.

Education

With regard to educational provision for people with significant physical disabilities, the major developments of the past decade have been progressions of the movement towards 'mainstreaming' which has been in evidence particularly since the early 1970s. One of the most notable changes has been that people with significant physical disabilities are now much less likely than previously to attend segregated special schools and crucially they are also being facilitated in formal ways to sit for state examinations at post-primary level. For example, an amanuensis is allowed to write the answers if the examinee's speech is not intelligible on cassette recordings and a time allowance is granted where speed of writing is hampered by physical disability and where a typewriter, word-processor or tape-recorder could not be used.

The whole question of access to third-level education for people with physical disabilities has been opened up very much particularly since 1990 with the establishment of the Association for Higher Education Access and Disability (AHEAD). AHEAD is supported by the Higher Education Authority and funded in part from European Union sources. It has been strongly to the fore in raising awareness of the social and physical barriers which need to be removed if people with physical disabilities are to gain full access to third-level education.

While there have undoubtedly been enormous improvements in terms of educational provision for people with physical disabilities since the 1940s – the earliest school days of the people interviewed for this study – it is clear from a number of sources that major shortcomings still exist in this core area. For example, the Report of the Special Education Review Committee (Department of Education, 1993) and the Working Group on Education for the Commission on the Status of People with Disabilities(1995) have highlighted the following as being among the many ongoing barriers to the real inclusion of people with disabilities in this sphere:

- Lack of legislation

- Poor physical access

- Limited geographical spread of provision of specialist educational support services, particularly at second-level

- Shortcomings in appropriate transport provision
- Lack of appropriate desks and equipment
- Lack of appropriate training of teachers
- Limited availability of aides to deal with pupils' personal care needs.

Training and employment

The whole subject of training and employment has been very widely discussed in Irish society generally over the past decade and this has been due in large part to the high unemployment rates which have prevailed during this period. The employment situation of people with disabilities, in particular, has tended to be very poor and the rate of unemployment within this broad category has been estimated at 70 per cent (NRB, 1994). It is not surprising, therefore, that a number of initiatives have been put in place since the mid-1980s aimed at dealing with this overall situation. The significance attached to finding ways of improving training and employment opportunities for people with disabilities was highlighted in the early 1990s when the National Rehabilitation Board established a cross-representative, policy-making body, The National Advisory Committee on Training and Employment, to make recommendations in this area.

In the field of training, much attention has been paid to the issues of improving the quality of training available and opening up a greater range of training options for people with disabilities. With regard to improving the quality of training, one of the key developments has been the preparation by the National Rehabilitation Board, in consultation with service providers and people with disabilities, of a *Standard for Vocational Training*. European funding for training is now firmly linked to the quality of the training process and training outcomes and the new *Standard for Vocational Training* relates to training centres which are approved and accredited to deliver programmes under the European Social Fund. (European Social Funding is available only to training centres catering for people with disabilities deemed eligible for employment in the open labour market.) It is hoped that the *Standard* will ensure that the vocational training programmes provided for trainees with disabilities are of a quality equal to or better than those available to their non-disabled peers, so that they may be in a position to compete on equitable terms for suitable workplaces.

Attention has also been paid to ensuring that trainees with disabilities will receive certificates or diplomas on completion of their courses which will be recognised not only in Ireland, but elsewhere in the European Union. Mainstream certification has become increasingly recognised as an essential prerequisite for equality of access to the labour market, particularly at levels where competition is high.

The past few years have also seen a growing emphasis on training the trainers of people with disabilities. It is expected that in the near future every trainer involved in the implementation of ESF-supported training for people with disabilities will have a recognised qualification.

The main development in terms of mainstreaming in relation to training came in 1994 when FÁS, the National Training Agency, decided to introduce a range of special measures to promote the employment as apprentices of people with disabilities who otherwise meet the entry requirements for apprenticeship training. Discussions have also been in place between the National Rehabilitation Board and FÁS with the objective of increasing the participation of people with disabilities on a range of other mainstream FÁS training schemes.

On the *employment* front, there has been a renewed emphasis on the potential significance of the 3 per cent quota scheme for the employment of people with disabilities in the public service which was introduced in 1977 and which is widely agreed to have fallen far short of its stated objectives. A monitoring committee under the Central Review Committee of the Programme for Economic and Social Progress was established in 1992 to report on the operation of the scheme and the Government is committed in its Programme for the period 1993-97 to implementing the scheme in the public service and to giving serious consideration to the introduction of legislation for a quota throughout the economy. The National Rehabilitation Board (1994), among other bodies, has recommended that the 3 per cent quota in the public service should be enshrined in legislation, monitored and enforced with appropriate sanctions. In the private sector, there has recently been a new 'Positive to Disability' excellence symbol launched by the National Rehabilitation Board. This symbol of excellence, which is concerned with the recruitment and selection of employees with disabilities, has already been awarded to ten companies in Ireland.

Another key development of the past decade has been the emergence of 'supported employment' as a concept. The EU Horizon-funded Rapport initiative in the Midland Counties in 1987/88 was influential in terms of highlighting the potential of this type of approach. Essentially, that was an action research project which brought together committed employers and employees with a disability in a structured way to identify and find solutions to the barriers facing persons with a disability both before and during employment. Broadly speaking, 'supported employment' involves 'real work' in an integrated setting, which many of the respondents in this study identified as being so important, and the people with disabilities involved are paid the going wage through schemes such as the NRB Employment Support Scheme. That scheme applies to people whose productivity is between 50 per cent and 80 per cent of the standard. The employees are paid the full wage by the employer, who is then paid an employment support, which makes up the gap between the employees' assessed productivity and the standard productivity.

Sheltered work still remains the most likely option for most people with disabilities whose productivity is significantly below what is considered acceptable in open employment. In its Submission to the Commission on the Status of People with Disabilities, the National Rehabilitation Board (1994:46) pointed to the ad-hoc development of these workshops and recommended that:

> The status of people with disabilities currently in sheltered work setting be reviewed, including issues such as wage structure, the legal status of workplaces and workers, funding, standards and conditions.

The potential of teleworking as an employment option, particularly for people with physical disabilities, has been under investigation in Ireland in recent years through a number of projects funded under the EU Horizon initiative. While this could have major implications for the future, it has been noted by the National Rehabilitation Board (1994) that teleworking and other home-based options should not just be developed as a substitute for making working environments accessible.

Physical access

The crucial significance of environmental access for people with significant physical disabilities was raised over and over again by the people who participated in this study. It was clear from their accounts that major problems continued to exist in relation to this right up to the mid-1980s when the interviews were conducted. Since that time there have been two notable developments which have gone some way towards improving the situation or at least heightening awareness of it.

The first was the coming into force of Part M of the Building Regulations 1991. This applies to access for people with disabilities to public buildings. Its underlying philosophy is to 'ensure that, as far as is reasonable and practicable, buildings should be usable by people with disabilities' (Department of Environment, 1991). Part M provides for 'access and use'; sanitary conveniences, and audience or spectator facilities. In each of these areas the requirement is that 'reasonable provision' be made for people with disabilities. Part M of the Regulations applies only to new buildings or where substantial renovation or change is occurring. While the introduction of these Regulations was generally welcomed, there has been a good deal of disquiet over their limited scope and the poor monitoring arrangements associated with them.

The second significant development of the past decade has been the emergence of local access groups in cities and towns around the country. These have played a key role in raising awareness about environmental access at a local level.

Technical aids and equipment

The field of technology has arguably changed at a faster rate than any other sector of our society over the past decade and it, in turn, has impacted very widely on all spheres of life. New and more sophisticated technical equipment, which can make a very significant contribution towards the quality of life of many people with physical disabilities, is continually coming on to the market.

The National Rehabilitation Board established a Disability Resource Centre (DRC) in Dublin in 1993 and this has contributed towards raising awareness of the range of products on the market. The centre is linked in to the sophisticated and user-friendly computerised HANDYNET system which holds information on technical aids for 'easier living' on the European market. The DRC also displays a wide range of equipment, which people with disabilities can try out on the premises, and provides information on where such equipment can be bought, how much it costs, and whether or not there are any grants available.

It must be stressed, though, that there is a serious lack of resources to fund the purchase of even basic appliances, such as electric wheelchairs. This point was underlined in the Interim Report of the Review Group on Physical and Sensory Disability (Department of Health, 1992).

Residence and personal care

One of the points which emerged most strongly from the people interviewed in the study was that the options available in relation to meeting their residential and personal care needs were extremely limited. Essentially, they described a situation where they either lived in the community with support from family members or else they had to enter an institutional type of residential care setting. The lack of any real prospect of being able to live independently in the community without having to depend on family, and elderly parents in many cases, was a cause of huge concern for many of those interviewed and the prospect of entering residential care was absolutely dreaded by most.

The period since 1986 has seen some very exciting changes which have begun to open up this whole area of provision, an area which is so fundamentally important and which had seen so few developments over the previous decades. The first development of note has been the considerable expansion of the Home Care Attendant Service, first launched on a pilot basis by the Irish Wheelchair Association in 1983. The essence of this scheme is that it is available at unsocial hours, at short notice if necessary, and can be relied upon to provide a well-trained and competent service to people with significant disabilities and their families. It complements the services of the Public Health Nurse and the Home Help Service. The care attendant acts as a substitute for relatives to enable them to attend to whatever they want, or need to do.

A second important development, also associated with provision which pre-dated the mid-1980s, has been a considerable change in the extent and type of provision being made available under the auspices of the Cheshire

Foundation of Ireland. The number of Cheshire Homes in Ireland has increased from eight to eleven in the past decade and two further Homes are planned. The number of places has also increased and currently stands at approximately three hundred. What is particularly significant is that the Cheshire Homes are now moving firmly away from institutional provision to a more independent-living type of approach. For example, the new Homes which have been developed provide self-contained flats and bedsitters with some areas for communal activities. At present, the Foundation is also planning a two-year training course for people with physical disabilities, mainly those who are living in residential care, who wish to live more independently, with the help of Personal Assistants. This project, which is being funded under the EU Horizon Programme, was initiated following research into the views of people living in Cheshire Homes.

A third and particularly significant development relating to residence and personal care was the establishment by the Center for Independent Living (CIL) in Dublin of a two-year action research programme called INCARE. Funded under the EU Horizon Programme, INCARE was aimed at developing and researching, for the first time in Ireland, a consumer controlled personal assistant service. In its pilot phase, it involved twenty-six people with significant physical disabilities (referred to as leaders) and their fifty Personal Assistants (PAs). As well as being consumer controlled, the PA scheme differed from previous attendant schemes in Ireland in that each person with a disability had the services of a PA for a minimum period of twenty hours per week. The leaders employed and utilised the PAs in a variety of settings. These included: providing assistance in the home environment and in residential care, in the study place, in the work place and in the social and recreational environment. The PA's work varied significantly from leader to leader and depended on how the leader wished to avail of the help of his/her PA.

Training for both leaders and PAs was central to the INCARE programme. The leaders, through peer consultancy, were trained to understand and practise the philosophy of independent living. They were involved in empowerment and assertiveness training to enable them to take control of and responsibility over their lives and to be effective employers and trainers. The PA training programme, designed by the leaders, operated on two levels – 75 per cent in-service and 25 per cent in class. The training programmes were devised and operated in close conjunction with outside organisations including FÁS, the National Rehabilitation Board and the National College of Industrial Relations.

The INCARE pilot programme has generated considerable interest within the disability field and a Cross Departmental Advisory Group was established by the Minister for Health in 1995 to look into the future for such a service. Following the recommendations of that Group, core funding from the Department of Health has now been secured to enable those who were involved in the pilot scheme to continue to receive the service.

It is difficult to anticipate the future for CIL's Personal Assistant service as originally envisaged, since this entire field is developing at a very fast pace. However, what seems abundantly clear is that the notion of Personal Assistance, which has such potential for opening up the lives of people with significant physical disabilities, is here to stay. CIL itself now has thirteen satellite groups around the country and a PA service is currently being developed using the FÁS Community Employment Schemes. It is also lobbying hard for the setting up of an Independent Living Fund which would enable people with significant disabilities to have access to a more flexible and secure PA service than is currently available.

Concluding Comment

It is quite clear from the various developments of the past decade, which have been outlined above, that people are beginning to think differently about significant physical disability and the needs and potential of people who are either born with disabilities or acquire them during their lives. The changes which have been put in place have probably come too late to have any major impact on the lives of some of the older people in the study and others of their generation. However, the younger people and especially those who have managed to secure an all-important second level education may well come to benefit from some of the fruits of these ongoing developments. It would certainly be interesting and informative to have the opportunity to follow up on the lives of the thirty people who took part in the study.

It should, of course, never be forgotten that the improvements of today have many of their roots in the determination and concern of people with disabilities, people like Paula, who have already suffered at the hands of the system:

> What I want to do is to help others that are coming on after me; to make it more helpful to them by knowing what I had to put up with so as they wouldn't have to do the same.

Appendix

Brief descriptions of the main features of cerebral palsy, traumatic spinal cord injury and multiple sclerosis are presented below. They have been compiled so that the experiences of the people discussed in this book can be more fully understood and, as such, are not intended for wider use.

Cerebral Palsy

Cerebral palsy is not a specific disease. Rather, it is an inclusive term which refers to a group of disorders characterised by abnormal control of movement or posture, early onset, and the absence of recognised underlying progressive disease. The cause of cerebral palsy may be an injury to the brain before, during or after birth. The significance of hereditary causes remains somewhat unclear but these are generally considered to be relatively unimportant particularly as single factors giving rise to the disorder.

The prevalence of cerebral palsy is about 2 per 1,000 live births. It occurs more frequently in males than females. The percentage distribution for males and females is about 60 per cent and 40 per cent respectively.

The usual initial complaint in children with cerebral

palsy is failure to meet early developmental milestones. Such failure may be the manifestation of many conditions and a diagnosis of cerebral palsy can only be made after the possibility of various other diseases and disorders has been ruled out. The diagnosis of cerebral palsy does not have the precision and accuracy of many medical diseases and is made principally on the basis of clinical examination.

There are various forms of cerebral palsy depending on the site of the brain damaged. Spastic cerebral palsy is by far the commonest and accounts for approximately 70 per cent of all cases. It is a condition in which there is marked rigidity of movement and an inability to relax muscles. Athetoid cerebral palsy, another main type, is characterised by an involuntary distortion of attempted movement so that it is uncontrolled and uncoordinated. Athetosis usually affects a number of different parts of the body and the arms, legs, facial muscles, lips, tongue and throat may all be involved.

The motor dysfunction associated with cerebral palsy ranges from being very mild in some cases to being very severe in others. Although motor dysfunction is the defining characteristic of cerebral palsy, other disabilities are often present. Mental retardation is among the most significant of these and is found in at least half those with the disorder. Other dysfunctions which may be associated with cerebral palsy include: visual defects, impaired hearing, and speech and learning defects.

The treatment of cerebral palsy, particularly during childhood and adolescence, is commonly based on inputs from various professionals including doctors (especially paediatricians, orthopaedic surgeons, and eye and hearing specialists), physiotherapists, speech therapists and psychologists.

Traumatic Spinal Cord Injury

The spinal cord is hugely significant in human anatomy for two main reasons. Firstly, it is the main transmitter of all impulses and messages from the brain to all parts of the body and vice versa. Secondly, it is a nerve centre in its own right, controlling vital functions such as voluntary movements, posture, bladder, bowel and sexual functions as well as respiration, heat regulation and blood circulation. A severance or severe injury to the spinal cord always results in significant disability from the site of the lesion downwards. Spinal impairment may arise from either acute injury or from disease. Our concern here is with impairment due to traumatic injuries.

Road traffic accidents are consistently found to be the main causes of over 40 per cent of traumatic spinal cord injuries in industrialised countries and falls tend to account for a further 20 per cent approximately. Other major causes include industrial, agricultural and sporting accidents as well as acts of violence.

Figures for rates and prevalence of traumatic spinal cord injury in Ireland are not available. The estimated annual incidence of this condition in the United Kingdom is 10-15 per million. Traumatic spinal cord injury can be sustained at any age. However, it has been found that such injuries occur most frequently in people aged between fifteen and twenty years. It is a markedly male condition with a male/female ratio of three or four to one.

The diagnosis of injury to the spinal cord is usually obvious with the only question being the nature and extent of the injury. The most common means of describing a spinal cord injury is to state whether it is a complete or incomplete lesion at a given level of the spinal column. A complete lesion means a complete lack of sensation and motor function below the level of the injury. An incomplete lesion means that the injured person will have only certain degrees of sensory and/or motor function below the level of the lesion.

Considerable emphasis is placed on the emergency phase of care for the person with suspected spinal cord injury as mishandling can lead to a significant worsening of both complete and incomplete injuries. People with suspected spinal cord injuries in Ireland are generally treated at the Spinal Injury Unit attached to the National Medical Rehabilitation Centre in Dublin.

Hospitalisation following traumatic spinal cord injury tends to be of relatively long duration. The majority of people are hospitalised for between six and twelve months.

Those who sustain traumatic spinal cord injuries often receive additional injuries like major bone fractures, head injuries and lacerations in the traumatic incident. Medical complications associated with the condition include urinary tract infections, pressure sores, spasticity, pain, respiratory problems and difficulties with body temperature regulation.

People with spinal cord injuries are generally treated by a team of professionals drawn from different disciplines. It is common practice for them to be re-checked annually and to be hospitalised for this if necessary.

The life expectancy of people with traumatic spinal cord injuries has been significantly extended over the past few decades as a result of developments in drug and surgical techniques and improvements in rehabilitation.

Multiple Sclerosis

Multiple sclerosis (MS) is a neurological disease that attacks myelin, the multilayered sheath of protein and fat that is wrapped around the message carrying fibres in the brain and spinal cord. Over time, scars form in the areas of myelin destruction causing nerve impulses to be slowed or interrupted. This process results in the symptoms of MS which vary according to the location of lesions and thus from person to person. Some of the common symptoms include incoordination, muscle weakness, fatigue, difficulty in walking, numbness, double vision, tremors, spasticity, urinary and bowel problems and slurred speech.

At present, MS is incurable and its cause/s remain unknown in spite of being the subject of considerable research attention. It has been found to be unequally distributed in geographical terms. Its frequency increases with distance from the equator in both the northern and southern hemispheres. Ireland, with a prevalence rate of 65.5 per 100,000 population has been identified as a high frequency area. The disease has been found to occur more frequently in females than in males – an average ratio of three women to two men with the diagnosed condition.

The onset of MS is predominantly between the ages of twenty and fifty. The risk of developing it rises steeply with age from early adolescence, reaches a peak in the thirties and forties, and then declines steeply until it becomes quite remote after the age of sixty. The onset may be either sudden or insidious. The diagnosis of the disease, which is difficult because of the diversity of its signs and symptoms, is undertaken on the basis of clinical tests supported by an increasing range of technical examinations.

The variability of the course of MS is one of its key

characteristics. It tends to be marked by a sequence of relapse and remission and the severity of symptoms can vary very much even within one day. The impact of the disease on life expectancy is difficult to determine because of such problems as identifying the time of onset of the disease. The average duration of the disease in fatal cases has been found to be between thirteen and twenty years. However, it is known from individual case reports that it can run its course in a few weeks or persist for over sixty years.

The medical management of MS is generally agreed to be particularly problematical because both its cause/s and cure are unknown and because of its unpredictable course. The main emphasis of available therapies is on trying to relieve symptoms.

REFERENCES

Commission on the Status of People with Disabilities (1995), *Update,* No. 2.

Department of Education (1993), *Report of the Special Education Review Committee* (Dublin: Stationery Office).

Department of the Environment (1991), *Access for Disabled People, Building Regulations, 1991, Technical Guidance Document M* (Dublin: Stationery Office).

Department of Health (1992), 'Review Group on Physical and Sensory Disability: Interim Report to the Minister for Health' (Unpublished).

National Rehabilitation Board (1994), *Equal Status: Submission to the Commission on the Status of People with Disabilities* (Dublin: NRB).